CHILDREN OF NOAH

BEN LUCIEN BURMAN HAS ALSO WRITTEN

EVERYWHERE I ROAM

ROOSTER CROWS FOR DAY

MIRACLE ON THE CONGO

BIG RIVER TO CROSS

BLOW FOR A LANDING

STEAMBOAT ROUND THE BEND

MISSISSIPPI

Children of Noah

GLIMPSES OF UNKNOWN AMERICA

BY

BEN LUCIEN BURMAN

Drawings by ALICE CADDY

JULIAN MESSNER, INC.   NEW YORK

PUBLISHED BY JULIAN MESSNER, INC.

8 WEST 40TH STREET, NEW YORK 18.

COPYRIGHT 1951 BY BEN LUCIEN BURMAN.

PUBLISHED SIMULTANEOUSLY IN THE DOMINION

OF CANADA BY THE COPP CLARK COMPANY, LTD.

PRINTED IN THE UNITED STATES OF AMERICA.

BOOK DESIGN BY EDGARD CIRLIN

FOR FRITZ DASHIELL
WHO WAS THE PATIENT GODFATHER
OF SO MUCH OF THIS BOOK

A BIT OF CHRONOLOGY

For those who are curious about such matters, the factual chapters here, which appeared in the *Reader's Digest*, the *Saturday Review Of Literature*, the *Virginia Quarterly*, *Holiday*, and *Collier's*, were all written since 1945. *Fiddle Tune* is also of very recent date. The three mountain ballads toward the end of the volume, on the contrary, are almost the first writings of mine to be published, being originally printed by Carl Van Doren in the old *Century Magazine* during the Twenties; *Ballad of Piny Ridge*, 1924, *The Cobbs and McFarlands Are Fightin'*, 1925, *Oh, They're Seekin' Jamie Tolliver*, 1926. I hope they may still have a little interest for the reader. The other verses are folk poetry I have heard in my river traveling. *Children of Noah*, published in the old *Pictorial Review*, is the only short story of mine I care to see reprinted. Though it is, of course, fiction, its characters, with only a few superficial changes due to the passing of time, seem to me as basically representative of the region as when the story was written in 1927.

BLB

CONTENTS

INTRODUCTION

As I travel about the various regions of our country, and observe the infinite variety of its peoples, I am constantly struck by a miracle—the miracle of how the nation holds together. For the individuals who comprise it are often totally different in their ways of thinking and acting; they know as little of each other as though their neighbors were on Mars.

This was brought home to me most forcibly early in my writing. Born in the Mississippi Valley, I had known about shantyboatmen from my earliest childhood; a shantyboat was as familiar to me as a taxicab to a hotel doorman. Yet when in the early Twenties my first story about a shantyboat was published, I received a number of indignant letters denouncing me roundly for having created such a preposterous fiction and then trying to pass it off as fact.

There are those at this moment in Eastern literary circles, who having spent all their lives among the sophisticated, cannot believe that simple country people still exist in parts of the South, much as they existed many years ago. I have never discussed the latest fads in writing or criticism with the shantyboaters of the Mississippi, but I am quite sure they would find equally incredible and baffling a description of some of the queer characters I have encountered who make a living fishing in the waters of literature.

We form our judgments by those things with which we are familiar. The Pygmies whom I met up the Ubangi River in Africa, when brought to Brazzaville, the capital of the area, were astounded to see white children. Having known only white adults in their fever-ridden wilderness, they had firmly believed that all white people were born grown up.

I was very lucky in my birthplace. The careless traveler passing through Covington in Kentucky may not find it much different than the ordinary small city so familiar to most Americans. But to me as a boy its advantages were beyond price. Situated at the junction of the Ohio and the Licking rivers, almost the first thing I can remember is the whistle of the steamboats on their way from Pittsburgh to New Orleans, or the playing of the calliope of the *Island Queen*. One of the earliest sights I can recall is the tall, silent mountaineers being brought by the federal marshals to face trial for moonshining; the approaches to the Cumberlands were only a short distance away. At the edge of town was the Latonia race track; each year during the season the streets would be filled with picturesque gamblers, their gaudy-striped clothes further ornamented by dice cuff buttons and horseshoe tiepins studded with huge diamonds. Each Saturday I could go to the market-house and hear some half-blind minstrel, wandered down from the hills, singing the doleful ballad of *Pearl Bryan* or *Barbary Allen,* much as he might have sung in an ancient Scottish hall. What more could a hopeful author ask?

Those who are born in the Mississippi Valley, whether in the lowlands or the mountainous headwaters, have another advantage, though this may seem of dubious value to the outsider. We are all members of the grand fraternity of the flood; we are all children of Noah. Every year in Covington there was certain to be a small flood, and every few years there was a bad one. I know of nothing except a war that can turn a man more quickly into a philosopher. A flood is the great leveler. It spares no one, rich or poor; like the flood of Noah it is the great washer away of the sins of mankind. The sight of a raging flood river sixty miles wide, with the rain still coming down in torrents, and no one to say where the rising waters will end, is the enemy of the smugness that comes with false security. Noah would have made a first-class Mississippian. The Bible relates that his flood lasted almost a whole year.

I am afraid I have always been a tramp. If I remain fixed for a month or two, I begin to fret. My wife also has been corrupted, though her tastes originally were otherwise; she is now of the same gypsy disposition. We even changed the temperament of our cat, whose tribe, the feline sages say, is more attached to places than to people. Puss, who traveled many thousands of miles in car and steamboat, became even more vagabond than his keepers. If work held me anywhere longer than a week, he would grow restless and impatient. He would pace up and down on his fluffy paws, and remark in a manner even the dullest could understand: "O.K. This is getting tiresome. How about a little trip to New Orleans?"

The present collection is the result of my journeying. These are the stories of some of my friends of the rivers and the hills. For the most part, they are stories of little people, the millions of little people the visitor never sees as he stays in his commercial hotel in the heart of Memphis or Baton Rouge. They are the people that form the backbone of the South.

What has fascinated me as a writer is the childishness of the human being; how the individual will often devote his life to the pursuit of some absurd trifle. Let the reader look about him and he will find this a universal truth, whether a man be cotton picker or preacher, roustabout or college president.

I remember when I first made this discovery.

I was traveling through the Kentucky mountains some thirty years ago and happened to stop at a village in a region noted for its fiddlers. Hearing of an exceptional musician who lived some distance up a near-by creek, I engaged as my guide and companion for the trip an old man called Captain who was attached to the shabby hotel, a striking figure still over six feet despite his age, and possessing the beard of a biblical patriarch. We set out on horseback, and arrived at the crossroads store of which my violinist was the proprietor, a lanky, quiet man named Jake Tolliver.

As Jake took out his fiddle and made ready to play, Captain looked about the establishment with curiosity.

He turned to me suddenly. "Brother, do you like stick candy?" he demanded.

"Yes, Captain, I like stick candy alright," I answered.

Captain's eyes fixed themselves on a glass case near the door. "Brother, how about some stick candy?" he said.

I asked Jake to take care of his needs.

Captain accepted the two peppermint sticks the proprietor lifted from a jar, and thrusting one into his mouth, tucked the other into a pocket. "Put this away for the old woman," he remarked.

The stick he was chewing was soon finished. His eyes strayed to the case again. "Brother, do you like mixed candy?" he asked me.

I agreed that I liked mixed candy as well as peppermint.

"Brother, how about some mixed candy?" he inquired.

I told Jake to supply his wants again. Captain selected a black gumdrop from the bag the grocer gave him, popped it into his mouth, and stretching out on a counter, fell fast asleep.

Jake played for several hours, and it was time for me to go. I roused Captain, and mounting my horse, set off with him on the return journey. It was midsummer, and the creek bed that served as our highway had been empty of water for weeks. The dust choked our nostrils.

Captain cleared his parched throat. "Brother, do you like pop?" he demanded.

"Yes, Captain, I like pop alright," I replied.

"Brother, how about some pop?" he asked.

I agreed that when we returned to town I would stop at the general store on the square and buy him a bottle of strawberry soda.

It was dark, however, when we arrived. The store was closed, and Captain was compelled to hurry off to his duties as dishwasher at the hotel. I left at dawn next day without meeting him again, and did not return until some three months later. This time I stayed with the editor of the little county newspaper, and so was deprived of Captain's company. But I went to the hotel for lunch, and was standing on the porch, when Captain wandered out of the kitchen and saw me.

He came hurrying over. "Howdy, brother, howdy," he murmured. He shook my hand.

"Brother, how about that pop?" he said.

I have been writing about people who like pop ever since.

CHILDREN OF NOAH

MISSISSIPPI FISHERMAN

You want to know who I am?

Oh, I'm a shantyboat man

—RIVER SONG

MISSISSIPPI FISHERMAN

Long Jeff leaned over the edge of his shantyboat and began stroking his hand in curious fashion just under the surface of the muddy river where his little craft was anchored. He continued this action for some time, stopping now and then to look fixedly at the water.

A fat boy, who was sitting on the bank near by, eating an apple, watched the shantyman in wonder. "What you doing, Jeff?" he demanded.

"I'm petting a cat."

The fat boy spat an apple seed and looked at the shantyman in disbelief. "You ain't got a cat that can live under water, have you?"

"This ain't a mouse-catching cat." Jeff's voice was a drawl, as lazy as the movements of his body. "This here's a Red

River cat. A catfish. Red River catfish ain't like other Mississippi catfish. They just loves to be petted."

He bent over the shanty edge again and stroked his hand in an ecstasy of petting. "I ain't seen this cat for a couple of weeks now, I reckon. He's mighty glad to get back home."

The fat boy shook his head in bewilderment. "There's sure funny things in the river," he murmured.

There are very funny things in the Mississippi, as well as on the willowed shores along which it flows. In only a decade there have been many changes. Yet the river continues a rich treasury of American folkways and character. It is still a world of delight and wonder.

The old packet boats have vanished. In their stead have come huge new towboats, pushing their barges lashed together in great floating islands half a mile long. The river, like ancient China, absorbs these foreigners and at once begins to cast them in the accustomed mold. The young men who have taken the place of the old pilots on the new river monsters equipped with automatic stokers and radio eventually will succumb to the spell of the river. If they remain, in a few years they will become mellow, humorous, like the old-time rivermen, but wearing a different suit of clothes.

There is one river figure, however, who has survived almost without change to the present, and has thus become unique in the mechanized America of today; he is the Mississippi fisherman, like the drawling Long Jeff who pets catfish.

In spirit and often in appearance he is reminiscent of the pioneer carrying his rifle when the West was a wilderness. He is far removed from the world of the moment, with its monstrous automobile plants and its giant steel mills whose smoke darkens the skies. His life is a tranquil oasis in an age of turmoil where man has not yet learned to master the machines he invented. For the Mississippi fisherman is a rebel against mechanization and regimentation, as were the pioneers of an earlier time he so closely resembles. And like the pioneer, he is a deep philosopher who has found by living close to nature a partial key to the happiness sought by all humanity.

His type is of wide variety, ranging from the lanky Anglo-Saxon fisherman of Black or Red River to the merry Cajun of the bayous. But his creed and his way of life are always the same.

A philosophic attitude is a basic necessity for any Mississippi fisherman. For his fortunes are erratic and unpredictable as the winds which blow from the stormy Gulf. One week, when the shrimp weigh down his nets, or the catfish and buffalo bite as fast as he can bait his hooks, his pockets will be bulging. The next six months he may lack even the few pennies necessary to buy the meal to make his corn bread.

Years ago when I first traveled the river, the fishermen were scattered everywhere along the banks. Now, with the growth of industry along the northern reaches, they are concentrated mostly in Louisiana. One of the largest groups centers about Jonesville, pleasant little town halfway down the state, which glories in the title, the fish capital of inland America. Like all Mississippi fishing settlements, it is a place

full of character—and characters. As the traveler wanders about, seeing the tall, grizzled figures in their boots and ten-gallon hats who have come in from the countryside, he might imagine for a moment that he was walking down the main street of a mining town in the heyday of the West. The timid soul might believe that some of the swarthy passers-by were members of a gang of desperadoes, grim and dangerous. Actually they are the kindliest of men, who like nothing better than to joke with friend or stranger; there is everywhere a warmth and hospitality that cannot fail to charm the most cynical.

There are four rivers at Jonesville. Here the Tensas, Little River, and Ouachita come together to form the Black. All are full of the succulent catfish and the huge buffalo. The inhabitants say there are as many fishermen as fish, and of more unusual varieties.

I was strolling about one afternoon, visiting some shanty-boats anchored near the town, when I saw an old man on the river bank, bent over the horny skin of an alligator gar-fish. As I watched he began scraping off the bony scales, and dropped them with care into a wooden trough.

I stopped to chat for a moment.

The old man halted his work, pleased to have a visitor. "Bet I got something here you never saw before, mister," he told me.

He held up the cracked garfish hide to which some of the scales were still clinging. "You know all that pretty jewelry and the other pretty things made of shells you see in those fancy beach places?" he demanded.

When I answered in the affirmative, he tapped the fish hide with a significant finger. "Right here's where they all come from. Right from these old garfish scales."

He looked at the homemade racks where some other skins were drying, then surveyed the tiny cabin beyond. His wrinkled face lighted with pride. "Got a fine business here.

Only a couple of other fellows doing it in the whole world, I guess. Send the scales to Florida, Hawaii, all over. Sure is funny, getting all these pretty things out of a piece of ugly old gar hide."

He sifted some of the scales through his gnarled hands. "Each hide's got a bone that looks like a horse's head, and another's like a snake raising up to bite you. There's a beetle and a pelican and a chicken beak, too. They use the scales from the buffalo fish to make rose petals. You can't beat a fish hide for making pretty jewelry."

Most of the shantyboats which house the fishermen have gone from Jonesville to Cocodra Swamp on Red River, or found a place on the other smaller streams that wind through the neighboring wilderness. Numerous fishboats connect Jonesville with these tiny settlements, going out at frequent intervals to collect the catch.

A voyage on one of these odd vessels is like a trip through the African jungle. All day the traveler glides beside the vast, brooding forest, the trees bearing long festoons of Spanish moss with buzzards perched grimly on the branches. Now and then a cabin shows in a clearing or a shantyboat is moored to a tree, with half a dozen hoop nets piled on the near-by shore. A fisherman rows out and drops a load of catfish or buffalo onto the scales at the bow of the fishboat. The young pilot notes the weight, and dumps the catch into the ice-filled hold.

Occasionally there is a woman who has taken the place of

her ailing husband at the nets, now and then a Negro with limbs like Hercules. Always as the boat comes to a halt, the young pilot passes out the flour and canned goods or a gaudy lamp or pillow cover he had been asked to procure on a previous excursion. For here in the swamps, where there are no roads, the fishboat is still the only link with the far-off world of the towns.

The fishboats are an education in native American humor —and the river law.

I was traveling by fishboat one day toward Cocodra, when a lanky fellow passenger in tar-stained brown overalls and a battered Western hat that gave him the appearance of a sheriff on the Pecos, an individual known as Dollar Joe, began to expound on the niceties of the Mississippi dweller's code.

"When you're a fisherman first thing you got to learn is to let everybody live way he wants," remarked Dollar Joe, cutting off a generous slice from a plug of tobacco. "Ain't your business what he's doing, unless he crosses up his neighbors. I'll show you what I mean."

He chewed meditatively a moment. "Guess you heard about that fellow down here owned a couple of mighty good hunting dogs, and he'd sell 'em to some man that was going away. Like you know, the dogs was trained to come right back, and then he'd sell 'em all over. We didn't do nothing to that fellow. We figured that was kind of like horse trading."

He spat with perfect accuracy at a passing turtle. "Well, a while ago a fellow come here with his wife on a shantyboat, from somewheres up in Missouri, he said. And he done the same thing like the fellow with the dogs, only he done it with his wife. She was a pretty woman, good cook, too, and every new fisherman that come in here didn't know nothing, the Missouri fellow'd trade his wife to him for his nets and his shantyboat. The woman'd stay with the new man a couple of weeks, and then say she was mad at him, and go back to

her husband. Well, we talked it over. And we figured that fellow was sure crossing up his neighbors. We got ways of fixing people like that on the river. One night when they was asleep we cut the lines tying their shantyboat to the shore, and just let 'em drift down the river. On the river you don't need no judge or no sheriff. Cutting a line's best kind of law there is anywhere. Too bad, ain't it, you can't cut the lines of people you want to get rid of in a town?"

Cocodra is typical of a Mississippi fishing settlement. A long row of shantyboats and cabins is set along the riverbank, some almost completely hidden by the cypresses. Beyond stretches Cocodra Swamp, a tangled, gloomy jungle, one of the last outposts of the almost vanished Mississippi wilderness.

Here and there are scanty fields for growing a little corn and potatoes and cotton; every fisherman in the region is a farmer as well. Occasionally there is a narrow earthen mound, higher than the roofs of the buildings; this is a refuge, where the few pigs and cows may find safety in floodtime. For Cocodra is overflow country, and all life has to be conducted with the knowledge that each spring the rains will swell the streams up the Valley, and the earth will vanish under a muddy sea. Even the houses are not like other dwellings. They are built on Choctaws, great hollow logs that rise slowly with the flooding water; when the tide recedes, the building comes down gradually once more to the land. Occasionally, if the house in its floating moments is not tied properly to a neighboring tree, there will be difficulty. I stayed once in a home on Choctaws where the kitchen, a separate structure from the main building, had been roped insecurely. When the waters fell and the dwelling came to rest, the kitchen was a full city block away. There it remained for an entire season, while the harassed women folk of the family carried the meals across the gap, until there came a new flood and the house was made whole again.

It is not an easy life, that of the swamp dweller. There is no electricity, and no running water. The only fuel is firewood, cut with an ax from the forest. Yet here the fisherman lives quietly, happily, much as his ancestors lived a hundred years ago. Each day he runs his lines and puts his catch in the latticed fish boxes showing before his cabin door; intent he waits until his keen ears hear the fishboat chugging down the river. Constantly he must patch the great rents in his nets, torn by a marauding garfish or a hungry alligator; regularly he must dip the tackle in his tar vats to keep the hemp from rotting. He is proud of his blackened hands.

"Ain't a good fisherman unless he's covered with tar," is a Cocodra proverb.

When he tends his little crops, it is often by the signs of the moon, in the ancient way of his forefathers. Again and again I have heard a fisherman farmer tell how, if he observes the signs in his planting, he can make his corn grow six or eight or twelve feet high, as accurately as though it were measured with a ruler; he can likewise at will make the ears appear high or low on the budding stalk. Almanacs which explain these lunar signs are still a treasure in almost every household.

Inseparable from the fisherman is his hound, here the famous Catahoula hog dog, an animal that legend crowns the undisputed king of the Mississippi swamps. They are sad, moth-eaten creatures, these Catahoulas, even more melancholy in appearance than the doleful bloodhound, bony as skeletons from their ceaseless chasing in the gloomy woods. The most prized of the breed bears a fabulous name, the "glass-eye, leopard type"; this is because of his faded spots, which suggest that some unhappy sire in the dim past might have been a bird dog.

Yet despite the animal's sorry appearance, his master regards him with affection and veneration. For the Catahoula is a vital part of the swamp dweller's life. The dog helps him hunt his coon and possum, and gives him comfort on his lonely vigils; he guards the swampman's wife and children, and warns them of the rattlesnake and the occasional panther. But most important of all he presides over the hogs.

Each spring, to save feed, the fishermen put out their hogs to forage in the wilderness. When fall approaches, there is a great roundup that covers all the swamp. It is the Catahoula hog dogs who take complete charge of the occasion. For several days they range through the tangled trees, where a man could never make his way. Working sometimes as a team, sometimes alone, with almost human intelligence they drive any hog they come upon to the pen of the nearest farmer, though the dog may be twenty miles from the point where he started. When all the pigs in the woods have been thus collected, the swamp dwellers make the rounds of their neighbors, and inspecting the crude brands, sort out their grunting property. Soon after, they put the animals in a little barge, and attaching a gasboat, start for their homes on the river; while the Catahoula sits serenely in the stern beside his master, content with a labor well done.

The women of the swamps, like their husbands, remind the observer of the pioneer folk who set out in their covered wagons for California. Patiently they go about their household duties, roasting their coffee, and baking their corn bread, often working in the fields when the male members of the family are busy at their tasks on the water. In their spare moments some sew fancy coverlets to lay over their handmade beds; others knit the hoop nets stretched out like giant spider webs before every doorway. They are self-reliant as the men, prepared to take over their husbands' duties in any emergency.

Some are unusually versatile, like my old friend Aunt Mollie, whom I visited on her shantyboat, neat as any parlor. Now nearing ninety, in her busy career Aunt Mollie had been fisherman and trapper, as well as Holiness preacher, midwife, and teacher for all her swamp-dwelling neighbors.

Her blue eyes still peered brightly out of her withered face, as she brought some coffee and crackling corn bread, and set them on a table.

"Yessir, people used to pay me a dollar a head to learn their children reading and writing," she declared. "Now they comes around some places in boats to git the children and take 'em to a regular school. Everybody says I could git a job quick in one of them new schools. They says them teachers gits paid plenty more a head than I was gitting for learning 'em. But I don't like living around a town."

There is a touching quality about many of these swamp dwellers, a simplicity that seems almost unbelievable in the stern world of today, where the great cities so often breed only aloofness and self-interest. On one occasion I traveled for several hours with a poor fisherman who at my request was taking me to a distant point in his rickety gasboat. When at the end of the long trip I asked how much I owed, he looked at me in surprise. "I couldn't charge you no money for that, brother. You and me was just having a good time talking."

And nothing I could do would make him change his mind. They are deeply religious, and even though they cannot read, always possess a large, much-thumbed Bible. When a literate stranger passes they are apt to ask him to quote and interpret some of the more familiar passages.

Sometimes they are so lost in the forest they are off the watery highway traveled by the fishboat and thus cannot have even the services of the wandering Holiness preacher.

Deep in the cypresses I found such an individual, a feeble, white-haired old man, living all alone on his tiny shantyboat, with only the low-circling cranes for his company.

I helped him raise his nets, and made ready to go.

He turned to me wistfully. "Brother, you ain't a preacher, are you?" he asked.

His face fell when I told him that I wasn't.

He shook his head sadly. "Brother, when you get to town, tell 'em to send me out a preacher, will you? I'm a-getting old and I ain't never been baptized. And I want to be baptized before I meet my Maker."

South of Jonesville and Cocodra lies another fishing area, the basin of the Atchafalaya, a wilderness that stretches from Red River to the Gulf. This is a bleak and melancholy region, where many an outlaw is said to be still roaming, with a high price on his uneasy head. So trackless are the swamps, so twisting the waterways, that years ago a steamboat was stolen from New Orleans and hidden in its recesses; to this day the vessel has never been discovered. Occasionally along a remote inlet, I have come upon some sinister figure tramping with gun on his shoulder, who avoids all the usual courtesies of honest men, and quickly disappears into the brush.

It was here that some years ago I met a fisherman who was a refugee from a famous Kentucky feud. Fleeing from the mountains as a youth after killing a man in a duel, he had found the sanctuary of the Atchafalaya, building himself a shantyboat, and tending his lines and nets with his neighbors. Now mellowed by the years, with all idea of combat long since ended, he thought more and more of the scenes of his boyhood. Hearing that I was a native of Kentucky, an irresistible longing seized him for the sight of someone who knew his home. He had traveled many miles to seek me out, and talk to me sadly of the piny hills he could never see again.

Most of the fishermen of the region, however, are like their fellows farther to the north, amiable souls, who seek only to wrest a living from the muddy rivers. They have the same daily problems, the same methods of fishing. These at times may seem odd to the unfamiliar visitor.

"Fish is gitting queer as humans," a dwarfish Negro who lived with his wife in a little cabin on Choctaws told me, as he baited his lines preparatory to going out in his boat. "Can't never tell what they're going to do nowadays. Used to ketch all my fish with doughballs. Now they won't eat nothing but P & G soap. All the fishermens around here ain't using nothing but P & G soap."

As the traveler moves into the southern reaches of the Atchafalaya, the scene begins to change, and so do the fishermen. The sun grows hotter. The Spanish moss thickens. It is the land of Evangeline, the bayou country of the Cajuns. Everywhere pirogues, the fisherman's swift craft that is a direct descendant of the Indian dugout, dart in silvery flashes back and forth across the glassy streams. Often from a shanty-boat door there drifts the sound of a voice speaking French.

These bayou fishermen are spread over much of lower Louisiana. A unique colony is found near the placid town of Plaquemine, where towering locks lift towboats from the Mississippi into the smaller waterways on their course to Texas. A narrow road twists and winds until it reaches a tiny ferry anchored in a stream known as Bayou Sorel. On the ferry is painted a cryptic sign: TRAVEL AT YOUR OWN RISK. NO DRUNKS AFTER 7.00 P.M.

The traveler, crossing on the awkward craft, comes upon a startling sight. A wide levee is built paralleling the bayou. In either direction, as far as the eye can reach, it is lined with the habitations of fishermen—houses, cabins, and shantyboats of every description, some floating in the water, and others pulled up on the land. A pile of nets and a tarpot stand on the bank near each picturesque dwelling; craft of all kinds, flatboats, gasboats, skiffs, pirogues, travel like a school of feeding minnows through the quiet water. Here and there a larger craft lumbers on its way, the vessel of a dealer, collecting the usual catfish and buffalo. Trucks, heavy laden with fishy cargoes, rumble down the levee, the drivers calling out jovially to the grizzled figures dragging their tackle across the sticky clay. It is a fisherman's paradise.

Most of the inhabitants are frontier types, like the dwellers at Jonesville and Black River and Cocodra; now and then there is a family whose deep-accented speech had its origin in a fishing village of distant Normandy. But a short distance down the vanishing road the inhabitants change abruptly. Here at Bayou Pigeon, the "End of the World," where the swamps begin to turn into the great Louisiana marshes, is a new fisherman's heaven. Here all are French, a gayer people than their Anglo-Saxon neighbors; a visitor speaking English

to the older generation would not be understood. In these few miles are two thousand fishermen, living as their fellows to the north, in a world apart.

As the Gulf comes nearer, the marshes stretch in all directions to the horizon. More fishing communities appear at the mouth of each lazy inlet. There are Frenchmen like those who were so busy one Christmas they could not stop their labors, and pious folk, unwilling to forget the day of the good infant Jesus, later celebrated their Christmas during Lent. There are Indians, and strange men dark with Spanish blood, and brawny Yugoslavs in their oyster camps, who drink tall glasses of orange wine, and talk of harvesting oyster crops as farmers talk of harvesting corn. There are the shrimp fleets, with crews from the ends of the earth, who sail their boats through heat and hurricane, and never ask the reason. Together they form a collection of colorful individuals whose like can rarely be seen in America.

The same simplicity of these Mississippi fishermen is often to be found in the little farmers who try to wrest an existence from their scant cotton patches along the river's shore. There are many of these poor farmers along the Mississippi, far too many; unequipped to carry on the battle in the harsh world of the machine, their difficulties sometimes leave them dazed, baffled. Yet they share the waterman's philosophy. They would trade their life for no other.

I shall never forget a tall, fine-featured old woman, clad in faded dress and sunbonnet, but with all the dignity of a figure from the Bible, that I saw one day sitting in front of her rickety cabin built alongside the great river. She had just received a letter; unable to read, she asked me to open the long envelope and tell her the puzzling contents. I took out the folded paper within, a tax bill from the local county seat; it informed her that for the year she owed the county and the sovereign state on whose domain we were standing the sum of two dollars and thirteen cents in taxes.

Her face grew bleak as she understood my words. "I knowed it was taxes," she murmured sadly. "I couldn't figure nobody else that would write me. Two dollars and thirteen cents. Where am I going to get all that money?"

She looked at the tax bill a long time without speaking. Her expression became a little more cheerful. "I don't know. Lord'll fix it up some way, I reckon. Maybe my boy that run off'll come back the way he done five years ago and pay it for me. Or maybe there'll be a flood that'll bring me a bale of cotton the way it done old Mace Jackson last year. A flood's mighty bad. But sometimes there's good things about a flood."

A huge towboat went up the river, pushing a vast floating island of barges. She watched absently. "Last year was a good flood for me. Them relief people give me flour and clothes, and a rich lady that seen me when she was a-doing the relief came back a couple of weeks after the flood was over and bought me a ice-cream sundae. That was a mighty fine day."

She folded the tax bill and put it carefully inside her dress. "Two dollars and thirteen cents. That's sure a heap of money. But I'll get along someways. Mississippi people always gets along."

KING OF STEAMBOATMEN

Landing keeper, did the "Belle" pass by?
Went down this morning like the moon before day
—River Song

KING OF STEAMBOATMEN

I FOUND him at Natchez.

For a long time my wife and I had been wandering up and down the Mississippi trying to locate our elusive quarry. It was back in the Twenties, and in those days there weren't many people interested enough in the river to have any information. Besides a steamboat doesn't move with the dull accuracy of a train. Finally we heard at Natchez he was due to arrive that night.

We sat in the lobby of the Eola Hotel and waited.

At three in the morning a long, melancholy whistle sounded in the distance. We wakened the cab driver dozing outside and drove down the steep slope to the wharf where a few decaying buildings were strung out along the river, all that remained of the once-celebrated Natchez-under-the-Hill. A small steamboat was moving toward the wharf, her twin smokestacks coughing up dense clouds of smoke and soot, her high paddle wheel splashing noisily. I could vaguely make out her name, *Uncle Oliver*.

A tall Negro roustabout standing on the bow tossed a line, and the little craft made fast. The captain came walking down the gangplank. I studied him closely. He was a man of average height, with the sturdy physique common to most men who spend their lives on the river. His walk was jaunty, his movements electric. He seemed supercharged with energy.

But it was his face which instantly caught my attention, as he halted to talk to the wharf boss standing beside a bale of cotton. His eyes, so blue I noticed their color even by the flickering lamp overhead, were bright, merry; his mouth was curved in a smile that radiated warmth and geniality. He was obviously a happy man, a lover of pleasantry and laughter.

My hopes rose and I asked a question.

He shook his head with regret. "Sorry, my friend. Can't take any passengers." His jerky phrases popped out like bullets from a friendly machine gun. "Just gave up my passenger license. Only freight now. If you were a cow I could take you. Sorry. Too bad."

His words were faintly touched with the accents of the Cajun country.

I tried to persuade him, and my wife joined in my plea.

44

Suddenly I saw his blue eyes twinkle. He started to move away. "Nothing to prevent my hiring you as crew. Guess I'll regret it. Heard about you crazy artists and writers. Probably put me in an asylum, too. Your wife's a stewardess. You're a deck hand. Going to work you both like the devil. Come on aboard."

These words were the beginning of a friendship that was to have a profound effect upon my life. The speaker was Captain Dick Dicharry, who was later to become King of Steamboatmen of the Lower Mississippi. In Captain Dick there was to be personified the great tradition of the river, carried in full flower to our own time.

We stayed aboard the *Uncle Oliver* that night, and many nights and days thereafter. We made a new trip and another. I had known and traveled the rivers ever since my childhood. But this little vessel possessed some peculiar quality which somehow seemed to bring me closer to the soul of the mates and the engineers and the black roustabouts, and the boats on which they labored. Captain Dick became my touchstone to the Mississippi.

Our friendship deepened over the years. And I never ceased to find some new phase of his extraordinary character. Ordinarily a man of peaceful ways, when his anger was roused he was like an exploding volcano. Possessing the courage of a lion, I am sure he would not have hesitated empty-handed to fight ten men holding machine guns if they were abusing a child or an old Negro. He was the idol of his friends, and the terror of his enemies.

His kindness toward the poor or unfortunate was perhaps his most striking quality. For generations on the river a bitter feud has continued between the patrician steamboatmen and the lowly shantyboaters who live in the floating homes moored along the bank. Some captains send their craft at full speed past a shantyboat, regardless of the fact that the waves from the huge propellers or paddle wheels may almost swamp the smaller vessel moored along the willows. For Captain Dick the contrary was always the rule. I have seen him bring the *Uncle Oliver* to a stop as it neared a shantyboat where some river dweller was cooking supper, because he did not wish to send the rabbit stew or catfish flying to the shanty floor. I have seen him keep the whistle of the *Oliver* silent, because in a little houseboat near by a shantyman's wife lay ill, and the sound might have roused her from a troubled sleep. I have watched him fix newspapers or magazines to sticks and toss them over the side to the shantymen waiting below in a rowboat. And I did not wonder when I learned that though other steamboatmen might sometimes complain of cargoes stolen or damaged by lawless shantymen, nothing ever happened to the cargoes of Captain Dick.

I saw his wrath as well. Once when his boat was again carrying passengers, there came aboard a rich, disagreeable young man from a Northern city, full of scorn for the old-fashioned ways of the river. Always the visitor was finding something new to criticize. The soot from the smokestacks was frightful, the cabins with their narrow bunks were impossible, the cooking was atrocious.

With each remark Captain Dick's temperature mounted. But the young man was a guest on his boat, and he forced himself to remain silent.

The climax came one bright July morning when the complaining traveler sat down in the dining saloon with the other passengers for breakfast. A Negro boy set before each guest a plate of bacon and sizzling fried eggs, together with a dish of steaming hominy grits.

The quarrelsome guest stared at the unfamiliar hominy, and demanded that he be informed of the dish's composition.

Politely Captain Dick told him how hominy was an old favorite everywhere in the South, and painstakingly explained how it was made from corn.

The visitor sneered when the captain finished. "Take it away," he commanded the black boy. "Up where I come from we feed corn to the mules."

Captain Dick watched the little Negro go off bearing the uneaten dish. He said nothing. But those of the crew that saw his crimson face knew that he was near apoplexy. Soon after he rose from the table, and went off to the ship's galley. He remained there for some time, talking quietly to the wrinkled cook.

Next morning the passengers filed into the saloon once more for breakfast. The Negro boy emerged from the galley, and again set before Captain Dick and most of the guests the usual sizzling eggs and bacon. But before the disagreeable youth he placed a dismal concoction made of brown, coarse-ground particles swimming in cold water.

The youth stirred the mixture with his spoon. "What's this awful stuff?" he demanded uneasily.

Captain Dick fixed him with a cold and glassy eye. "Got it specially for you," he answered. "Eat it or go hungry. It's bran. Down here we feed that to the hogs."

Once embarked on a course he thought right, nothing would swerve him, no matter what the consequences.

In 1927 a terrible flood swept the Mississippi Valley, the worst disaster in all its troubled history. Captain Dick at once took his steamboat and began rescuing people from their flooded dwellings, carrying them off to the refugee camps on the levees, or to towns safe in the distant hills. Relief was not organized in the efficient manner of today, with Coast Guard stations and their trained crews ready to spring into instant action. The loss of life in some areas was appalling. Captain Dick labored night and day—savior of the living, doctor of the sick, and preacher for the dead.

Often, as he took the *Uncle Oliver* across the raging water, he would come upon a farmhouse whose inhabitants had been cut off for a week or more, unable to get word of their plight to headquarters. Occasionally one of these families would be at the point of starvation, with the mother and several children stricken with fever and dying for lack of medicine. At such times Captain Dick would bring out some of the government supplies and drugs he happened to be transporting to a refugee camp, leave what he thought necessary at the flooded home, and go on his way again over the muddy sea.

The area, for the emergency, was under military law. A newly arrived army lieutenant, more familiar with regulations than with disaster, was in charge of one of the near-by depots. Chancing to learn of Captain Dick's actions, he summoned the river captain, and informed him that he was disposing of government property without the authority the regulations demanded. He warned that if the captain continued his practices, the lieutenant would order him court-martialed.

Captain Dick, exhausted from his continuous labor without sleep, listened, and point-blank refused to obey his commands.

More days passed, and he found more stricken families; again he gave them the supplies they needed so desperately.

Then one morning when the vessel docked near the depot the lieutenant commanded, a grim-faced soldier was waiting. "Want you up at headquarters," he announced.

Captain Dick hurried off with him up the muddy path. In a tent on the levee some high officers on a tour of inspection were assembled, sitting stiffly on camp chairs. The depot commander turned to the visitors, headed by a solemn, much-decorated general, and asked that drastic punishment be meted out to the offending riverman.

Captain Dick faced the stern dignitaries unafraid. "If I pass a man dying of hunger, won't ask if he's got the right piece of paper," he declared stubbornly. "Can't eat paper. Going to feed him, that's all. Won't stop unless you shoot me through the head."

He continued to speak for some time, growing more and more eloquent as he told of the scenes he had witnessed. When he finished each of the visitors came forward and shook his hand. He left the tent, instead of a criminal a hero, with power to distribute relief supplies anywhere.

It was perhaps natural that so picturesque a character as

Captain Dick should gather about him a striking collection of personalities. His crew was a fiction writer's dream.

There was Captain Charley, the senior pilot, humorous, scholarly, uttering some new profound observation about life or humanity with every turn of the creaking wheel. There was Barney, the genial engineer, who each day drank a bucket of water from the muddy Mississippi to preserve his robust health, and avoid any dangerous dealings with medicines and doctors. There were the Negro roustabouts, singing, laughing, shooting dice, answering to the fantastic nicknames current on the river, Dusty or Pin or Augustus Caesar, Hot Mouth or Toe or Yankee Doodle.

"Come here to me. Sing a song, Reverie," Captain Dick would call to a towering roustabout with a piece of burlap draped about his fine-sculptured head, so that he resembled an Arab in the Sahara.

The giant Negro would step forward and begin to chant in a bass so rich it would have graced an opera house:

> *I'm tired of rousting on a river boat.*
> *Don't do nothing but load and tote.*
> *Got a girl in Atlanta*
> *Got a girl in Tennessee,*
> *Got girls all over*
> *But they ain't got me.*

Captain Dick would give him a coin and nod in approval. "Good singer. Like a lively boat. Won't keep a roustabout that can't sing."

She was a small vessel, the *Uncle Oliver*, and by no stretch of the imagination a pretty one. Paint was peeling like sooty snowflakes from her walls; one rusty stack had been damaged in a hurricane, and was leaning far from the perpendicular. Yet as she moved from New Orleans to the rich port of Greenville in the Delta, there was about the little boat a real nobility. For she was the fulfillment of an ideal.

Born in the village of Smoke Bend, Louisiana, as a boy Captain Dick watched with awe the white-painted river craft gliding down the Mississippi. He decided there was only one thing in life worth doing; he would become the proprietor of a steamboat.

His family, like most families, was amused and highly skeptical. But they offered little opposition when one day, become a young man, he announced that he was leaving home to find a job on the river.

The glorious era of the Mississippi steamboat had ended. The river trade was now in the last stages of decay, a condition brought about by the growth and ever-intensified competition of the railroads. Only a few vessels were left, struggling desperately with the giants of the rails for a perilous survival. These steamboats were always in need of a painting. Their railings were chipped, and their roofs needed tarring. The windows of the cabins were cracked and broken. But to the young man from Smoke Bend, they were floating castles, full of wonder and beauty.

After much searching, he found a vacancy at last on a

vessel of the Bradford Lines, where the crew was lacking an assistant clerk. He persuaded the captain to give him a trial at an almost invisible salary.

For a week he lived in terror that the dreaded captain would change his mind, and order him and his suitcase ashore. With joy on the seventh day as he went to the tiny office he heard the master say he was definitely hired. By the end of the month, his salary was quadrupled. The boy from Smoke Bend was launched on his career.

The Bradford boat was in the bayou trade, running from New Orleans to Houma, a French settlement drowsing in the shade of the spreading live oak trees that grew along the water. The cargoes were varied, mostly rice and fruit and vegetables that flourished in the rich soil, sometimes sacks of sugar from the great refineries. It was in this bayou steamboating that Captain Dick received his education as a riverman. It was a rough-and-tumble life, steamboating at its most difficult. The wandering streams, so close to salt water, were even more unpredictable than the hazardous Mississippi. A bayou might be thirty feet wide and the vessel traveling it twenty-nine; a projecting tree root would mean a barrier to be cut away with saw or ax. At times the stream would be so thick with mud, the vessel would seem to be a plow, cutting its way through a soggy field; now and then the channel would widen to a vast lake, where a sudden storm sweeping off the Gulf would threaten to send boat and crew to the bottom. Often the depth would shift in extraordinary fashion with a tide or unusual wind. A steamboat that anchored at noon beside some Cajun village in twenty feet of water, by sunset might find itself resting on dry land.

Despite the difficulties, Captain Dick's success was instant. Quickly he rose from assistant to a full clerkship; from time to time when there was need he began to act as master.

Always as the boat swung in for a landing he was the first to leap upon the muddy bank. Speaking the *gey-gey* French of the region with the fluency of a native, he would joke and banter for an hour if necessary with the muddy-booted farmers and the shrewd-eyed merchants waiting on the shore. Soon he possessed friends everywhere, who would often travel miles out of their way to bring him onions or yams or watermelons, or whatever the loads in their rattling wagons.

Then came the great day. He heard of a small steamboat up the river which was for sale at a bargain. Captain Dick had managed to save a little money from his salary. A local merchant who had confidence in the young riverman's ability offered to lend him the remainder. Captain Dick decided to buy the boat and run it on the Mississippi.

The decision was a bold one. The river trade was worse than before. Everywhere the railroads were undercutting water rates in a final desperate attempt to drive the steamboats out of business. But Captain Dick was not one to be deterred by danger. Soon the vessel, renamed the *Uncle Oliver*, was on its way from New Orleans up the river, carrying groceries and supplies to Greenville and the other river towns, returning loaded with bales of cotton. No landing was too small, too difficult. Sometimes the boat would stop to put ashore a farmer with a single grunting pig, sometimes it would take aboard a woman and her pig-tailed daughter, standing at night beside a signal fire as they waited to visit some relative down the valley.

Commanding the *Uncle Oliver* in the early days was a never-ending fight, battles with fog and storm and flood, but worst of all a battle to keep from sinking in the perilous seas of finance. It takes money to run a Mississippi steamboat, and with all Captain Dick's savings spent to purchase the vessel, there was no margin left to keep the boat in operation. It takes money particularly to pay for coal, and the *Uncle Oliver's* ancient engines ate coal as a hungry mule eats hay.

Once when his funds were less than nothing, the engineer came hurrying to Captain Dick to report an imminent catastrophe. The boat was in the middle of the Mississippi and still had several miles to run before it reached one of its regular landings; the engineer announced in ominous tones that there was not a single lump of coal left to feed the furnaces. In a few moments the boat, left without fuel, would start drifting helplessly down the river.

Captain Dick went below. A quick glance showed him the empty coal bins; with a practiced ear he heard the paddle wheel revolving slower and slower as the steam pressure fell in the boilers. Some roustabouts sat on barrels near by, watching him wide eyed, wondering what he would do.

He lost no time deciding. He snapped out some commands. "Come here to me, Reverie. Dusty, Alligator. Tear up this floor and throw it in the furnaces. We'll get that engineer some steam. Like he never had steam before."

The black men stood incredulous a moment, then seizing picks and axes, began ripping up the thick planks that formed the deck, and hurled them into the dying fires beneath the boilers. The dry wood crackled and leaped into flame. In a moment the furnaces were roaring. Clouds of smoke rolled out the lofty stacks, with now and then a dazzling shower of sparks, like an exploding comet. The paddle wheel turned faster and faster.

The vessel neared the landing. Captain Dick could hardly believe his eyes. On the banks stood a planter, waving his broad hat in signal. Near him stood a mountain of cotton, waiting for a steamboat. With a light heart Captain Dick watched the roustabouts roll the precious bales aboard and cover them with heavy tarpaulins. His troubles were ended, for this voyage at least; the cotton would pay many times over for the needed fuel. Soon the vessel was moored at a near-by coalyard, where the empty bins were filled to overflowing. The *Uncle Oliver* journeyed up the river, the monarch of the waves.

Disaster came to Captain Dick as it came to all rivermen. He met each trial with resourcefulness and courage. A terrible storm stove a great hole in the side and the vessel started to go to the bottom. By superhuman effort Captain Dick and his pilot managed to bring the boat to shallow water; when it sank at last, part of the Texas deck and the pilothouse still showed above the waves. Legend says that some neighboring farmers, seeing the sinking, rowed out to take off the bodies. Instead they found Captain Dick and a few of his crew sitting in water that rose above their knees, calmly playing draw poker on a floating table. The story happens not to be true. But it demonstrates how Captain Dick's gay spirit had captured the local imagination.

The sunken boat was raised and in a few months was running as before.

Captain Dick had owned the *Uncle Oliver* for some time when my wife and I first became his passengers. His period of prosperity was already beginning. His energy, his wide popularity, were bringing their natural results. Captain Dick and the *Uncle Oliver* were on the march.

With his success, it was logical that he should attract the attention of the steamboat's ancient enemy, the railroads. As the years passed the *Uncle Oliver* became the last packet in the once fabulous trade of the Delta. The railroads opened a bitter war to force him into bankruptcy, undercutting his rates on every occasion, trying in any way possible to persuade his clients to shift their freight from the river to the land. The master of the *Uncle Oliver* was far more now than an individual. He was the symbol of the Mississippi.

Captain Dick lost no time meeting the railroad's challenge. He sat beside me one afternoon in the pilothouse, his blue eyes alight with the joy of battle. "They say the steamboat's finished," he sputtered. "They say I'm—what's the name of the book?—*The Last of the Mohicans*. I'll show 'em. You watch. We're going to have some fun."

He began traveling about the river towns and the countryside, reminding the merchants and planters that wherever the competition of the river was ended, railroad rates always mounted to the sky. The local citizenry knew he spoke the truth from their own sad experience; they refused to be lured away. The railroad rates dropped lower and lower. But instead of taking away their trade the faithful Valley dwellers sent so much freight, the *Uncle Oliver* alone could no longer carry the burden; Captain Dick purchased a barge to keep the ancient vessel company. Still the freight increased, and the railroads fought harder. "Forced 'em to cut the cotton rate from four-fifty a bale to just a dollar," said Captain Dick proudly. "Not so bad for the boy from Smoke Bend."

More years passed and the *Uncle Oliver*, too old to struggle longer, went the way of all good rivermen and river boats. Captain Dick heard of a large packet for sale up the

Tennessee River, bearing the graceful name of the *Tennessee Belle*. He went off to inspect it, and concluding the purchase on sight, brought the vessel at once to the Mississippi. With pride he watched as it took its place beside the other ships at the busy docks of New Orleans. Here was no battered *Uncle Oliver*. The *Tennessee Belle* was a beautiful steamboat.

Captain Dick had loved the *Uncle Oliver*. But his feeling for the *Belle* was a profound devotion, intensifying with the years. And those who came to know her queenly ways could not fail to share his feeling.

A voyage upon her was an adventure in tranquillity. White painted like a bride she would glide over the brown river, while the ever-changing panorama of the Valley swept past her prow; the bandannaed Negro women working in the cotton fields, the farmers driving high-wheeled wagons overflowing with sugar cane. Her sweet-toned whistle would blow, echoing musically across the swamps and the levees. A child would run out from a shabby little cabin and shout in excitement: "Ma! Here she comes! It's the *Tennessee Belle!*" And Captain Dick's heart would beat a little faster.

The *Belle* was a success from the start. As time went on, like the *Uncle Oliver* she also became too small for her heavy cargoes. Captain Dick bought more barges. Residents of the river towns now shipped their freight by river as naturally as they drank their coffee at breakfast. The railroads, their previous campaigns a failure, changed their tactics; they tried to buy out Captain Dick, offering him many times the *Belle's* value. He laughed at their offers. The river was his life.

It was in meeting the emergencies always arising that Captain Dick found his greatest joy. He solved each new problem with ingenuity and master craftsmanship. Once a sudden shift of the river bottom caused the boat to ground on a sand bar where according to the charts there should have been ten feet of water. A quick fall of the river increased the difficulty. It was midsummer, and there was no hope of a freshet that would let the vessel float again. The situation seemed hopeless.

Captain Dick put on his boots, and dropping into the water that came up to his waist, walked about the stranded hull on a tour of inspection.

The captain of a ferryboat passing near by called out in sardonic sympathy. "You better start digging up that bar and plant yourself a good crop of potatoes, Dick. You'll have plenty of time to pick 'em. You won't get off till fall."

Other local rivermen, pushing a barge for a neighboring lumber mill or piloting a fishboat on its daily rounds, called out the same sardonic counsel.

Captain Dick paid no attention. All afternoon and all through the night he was in and out the river, directing some new attempt to set the *Belle* free. Now he started the huge paddle wheels to churning slowly forward, now he sent them thunderously rumbling in reverse, at the same time swinging the vessel back and forth like a pendulum to wear down the sandy bottom and let the boat pass. One moment he would be on the deck, directing the roustabouts as they shifted the cargo so that the stern would be lightened and a violent revolution of the engines might kick the boat across the obstruction; the next he would be working with a shovel in his hand, helping the black men dig away the sand that held her prisoner. Still there was no result.

Dawn came, and still the boat was motionless. Captain Dick and his men were exhausted. But they did not try to rest.

Captain Dick took down several of the hose lines set about the decks for use in case of fire. Ordering all the pressure the rubber would bear, he took one of the nozzles, and while others of the crew worked in similar fashion, began to wash away the sand beneath the prow. The noon sun rose overhead. Captain Dick and his men continued to ply the hoses, while the thick streams of water cut deeper and deeper into the sandy barrier. Suddenly the hull gave a curious quiver. The toiling Negroes shouted in triumph.

Captain Dick changed his water-soaked clothes, and rowing in his yawl to the little town down the river, went to a tiny restaurant perched on the bank, where the local pilots and mates were accustomed to assemble. Some boatmen were at a table, drinking coffee.

As Captain Dick found a seat, they gazed at him with their usual mock sympathy.

"Don't take it too hard, Captain Dick," said the ferryboat captain. "High water'll get here by Christmas. If you have good luck, maybe you can get her off by then."

The others echoed his gloomy prophecy.

Captain Dick made no comment.

Suddenly up the river there sounded the deep-toned whistle of a steamboat.

The rivermen listened in astonishment.

"Sure is like the *Tennessee Belle*," remarked the pilot of a fishboat, peering out the restaurant window.

The ferry captain nodded in agreement. "I'd swear it was

the *Belle*. But can't be the *Belle*. She's stuck tight as a dead turtle in the mud up at Two Mile."

The boatmen moved to the doorway to watch.

The whistle sounded again, then the *Tennessee Belle* appeared around a bend, majestic in the sunlight, the smoke from her towering stacks sweeping low behind her, like the black velvet train of a queen.

The boatmen took their places at the table again in sheepish silence.

The counterman chuckled, a drawling rustic from the swamps of Red River. "Can't keep them bayou steamboatmen grounded. Them bayou captains is half alligator, half frog. If they can't crawl off, they hop off. They'll do it every time."

"Hurry up with my black coffee," said Captain Dick.

The circumstances of Captain Dick's life changed sharply as he grew older. But there was no alteration in his picturesque character. Never did he lose his extraordinary appreciation of the Mississippi, its beauty, its poetry.

He could never understand a human being who did not love a steamboat. He was talking one day with a river captain, whose vessel in a near-by trade had been damaged beyond repair and was on its way to the steamboat graveyard.

Captain Dick expressed his sympathy to the former master.

To his amazement the other riverman, noted for his lack of warmth, only shrugged his shoulders. "What's a steamboat?" he demanded. "Just some deck boards, a paddle wheel, and a fool in a pilothouse."

Captain Dick grew hot with anger. "Thought you were my friend," he retorted. "Now I know better. You don't feel bad when your steamboat dies; I know you won't worry when I die. You're too cold a man for me. We're through."

Captain Dick had a story for every occasion. It was he who first made me aware of Old Al, the great alligator who is the

mythical king of the river; it was he who first told me how cross old steamboat mates become stubborn gray mules when they die, and how pilots turn into tall white cranes so that they can stand all day with their feet in the water, looking out over the Valley.

We would be sitting on the bow of the *Belle* at night when the pilot would suddenly blow a long whistle without apparent reason.

Captain Dick would peer down the dark river. "May be blowing for Captain Jeff. Guess you heard about Captain Jeff. Old steamboat pilot with a terrible temper. When he died they built a tomb on a bluff for him, with a little window. Then stood his coffin up on end so he could look out and cuss all the other steamboat captains going down the water. Rousters say if you don't whistle when you pass he'll sink you before the next trip."

Always he was a deep student of life, with an unusual curiosity about the world and its inhabitants. At times this led him into odd situations. Once the *Belle* was moving some convicts from the Louisiana State Penitentiary at Angola to a construction camp on a levee. Captain Dick noticed a well-dressed young man walking about the boat, and thinking him one of the prison officers, invited him to join the others at dinner. The young man refused with great politeness; Captain Dick soon learned that he was a trusty, serving a long sentence for safecracking.

Captain Dick was seized with an inspiration. In the ship's office was a heavy iron safe. Anxious to see a safecracker at work, Captain Dick asked the visitor if he could get it open; at his invitation, the convict began to twirl the dials.

"Had it open in half the time I could," Captain Dick related. "That was almost a bad mistake. Forgot there was over two thousand dollars in it. I slept on the money all night."

Often Captain Dick would have a pet aboard, at times a raccoon that would steal all the silverware and hide knives, forks, and spoons in some inaccessible hole, so that a cabin wall must be torn down before the loot could be recovered; at times it would be an enormous hog, grunting solemnly as it pushed aside roustabouts and firemen on the way to its favorite resting place beneath the boilers.

He was deeply attached to his crew, white and black; all were members of one great family. The feeling continued long after they had left the boat. Whenever the *Belle* landed, there was almost certain to be a Negro standing near the wharf who had once worked on the vessel, and was waiting to ask Captain Dick for a dollar that he knew would never be refused. When times were bad and jobs difficult to find, there were many occasions when Captain Dick hired roustabouts for whom he had no need in order to save them from going hungry.

In return the black men gave him a loyalty and affection that was close to adoration. They trusted him implicitly, even in their gambling.

I was down at the New Orleans docks with Captain Dick when one of his roustabouts came up solemnly, and announcing that he was about to start shooting dice with some local stevedores noted for their violence, asked Captain Dick for his assistance.

"After I been playing awhile, I'd mighty like it if you'd walk over to where I'm sitting and just kind of look at me, Captain Dick," he said. "I'll look back at you, and if I'm a-losing I won't say nothing. But if I've won a plenty of

money I'll git up and say, 'You a-wanting me, Captain Dick?'
And you'll say, 'Come here to me, Piece o' Man. I need you
on the *Belle* right now.' Then I goes off with you, and takes
all the money. If you don't come, them tough New Orleans

fellows won't let me git away till they've took back every cent
I won."

The devotion of the Negroes was at times embarrassing.
Once when Captain Dick fell seriously ill, some of the roustabouts who chanced to be Catholic attempted to burn so many
candles at a church altar the worried priest had to restrain
their piety for fear they would set the building on fire.

Year after year the *Tennessee Belle* continued to steam up and down the Mississippi. The Twenties became the Thirties, and the Thirties drifted into the uneasy Forties. I continued to travel on the vessel, sometimes in winter when sleet coated the decks and the willows on the shore were transformed into icy skeletons, oftener in summer when turtles basked in the sun on floating logs, and white cranes drifted over the water like flowers. And as I gazed out of the wide pilothouse window, I would remember what the *Belle* and the *Oliver* and Captain Dick had taught me of the river.

The *Belle's* end came suddenly a few years ago, when she burned off Natchez Island. Captain Dick retired to a farm not many miles from New Orleans. And to me the Mississippi has never been quite the same. Yet there would be none to deny that he had well earned his rest. The river for which he fought so valiantly was no longer forgotten. It was full of vessels now, giant towboats that pushed cargoes worth millions before their blunt prows. The Mississippi was carrying more freight than at any time in its long history. Captain Dick had bridged an era.

I visited him and his wife in their home shining white against the green Louisiana countryside. And now I am hoping his retirement is not permanent. For the house is built along the Mississippi levee. From its upper windows Captain Dick can look down onto the river, and see the smallest craft which moves across its muddy surface.

I was standing beside him in the barn, watching him milk

his favorite Jersey cow, called Sweet, when a great towboat came chugging up the water. Captain Dick's gaze shifted from the cow to the river; his busy fingers began to falter.

Suddenly over the topmost deck of the oncoming vessel a puff of steam arose and drifted away in a tiny cloud; the vessel blew a long salute.

In an instant Captain Dick had dropped the milk pail, and racing across the field separating him from the shore, dashed up the levee. His wife hurried to his side. On the distant boat the dimly seen pilot called out and waved his arms in signal. Captain Dick waved in return, and shouted an excited greeting.

"They salute this way day and night," his wife declared with a smile. She pointed off to a large electric bulb fixed outside the house. "When they blow after dark, he answers with the light. We don't get much sleep."

The towboat continued to steam up the river. Captain Dick watched it swing around a bend and vanish. His blue eyes grew thoughtful.

Off in the barn Sweet, the cow, mooed reproachfully beside the still-empty pail.

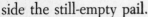

SHANTYBOAT VOYAGE

Buy me a pistol,
Shoot from town to town,
Going to shoot you, baby,
Jar your grandma down
　　　　　—River Song

SHANTYBOAT VOYAGE

WE SAT on the porch of the shantyboat, gazing across the dark river. Overhead the stars twinkled; beneath us the slow Mississippi swells lapped in lazy rhythm against the bow. Far up the valley a dull glow rose from the horizon, marking the lights of distant Memphis.

A rooster crowed somewhere beyond the willows on the bank. It continued to crow, loudly, urgently, its voice possessing a peculiar choking quality.

Big John, my shanty guide and companion, sitting near me in the shadows, listened. "Going to have bad news in the morning," he said. His voice was anxious. "When a rooster gets to hollering that way, crowing before his regular time, he's got what they calls hasty news—won't keep till daybreak. Hasty news is worst kind of news there is. We're sure going to hear something bad."

The cock ceased a moment, then renewed his odd announcing.

Big John's worry increased. "Trouble coming by morning sure," he declared. "My old woman told me I didn't have no sense going on this trip with you. Looks like she sure was right."

We went to sleep with the sound still echoing over the water.

We awoke at daybreak.

"Haven't heard that bad news yet, John," I remarked as we ate the breakfast of eggs and bacon he had prepared on the oil stove in our trim kitchen.

My lanky companion munched a biscuit thoughtfully. "It'll come all right. Maybe just a little late, that's all. I seen plenty of signs, good signs and bad signs. But hasty news is a sign I ain't never seen fail."

It was a comfortable little shantyboat, brightly painted in blue and white, with simple but pleasant furniture. I had rented it two days before from a river enthusiast as it lay in the harbor of the Tennessee metropolis.

We washed the dishes, decorated with fat cows munching in a bluish-tinted pasture; the china was already Big John's pride. We went out on deck.

Big John climbed into a gasboat, lashed alongside the shanty to form our motive power. I pushed at the bank with a wooden pole. The engine sputtered noisily. The shanty began to move slowly down the stream.

I took a place beside my companion at the rudder. Along the shore we drifted while the life of the great river unfolded before us in an ever-changing panorama. Fishermen sat in rowboats running their lines, taking from the hooks the catfish and buffalo they would later send off to a fish company in some distant settlement. On the porches of the shantyboats near by their wives were bent over battered tin tubs, engaged in doing the family washing. Occasionally we passed a gaunt figure standing beside a government light, trimming the wicks or polishing the lenses that guided the steamboats on their way to New Orleans.

A towboat steamed down the river, pushing a quintet of barges.

Big John chewed a cud of tobacco solemnly. "Here comes a old man with five wives," he mumbled. "Better watch him. Going to shake us up a little."

The towboat came abreast, and swung to make a crossing. Huge swells swept upon us. The shanty began a frenzied dancing. A great wave came into the gasboat, threatening to swamp us. A second and a third followed in quick succession.

The bottom of the boat was covered with a swaying yellow carpet.

A sudden gap appeared between the bow of the gasboat and the shanty as one of the lines linking the vessels whipped free. The gap grew ever wider. Big John tossed a new rope, and pulled mightily. The gap closed. The vessels were one again.

The river grew quiet.

I caught up a can and bailed out the water in the gasboat.

"Pretty big waves," I ventured, as I stretched out my wet feet to dry in the sun.

Big John spat in gaunt meditation. "You ain't seen nothing," he answered. "Wait till we meet the *Sprague*. Big Mama, they calls her. Biggest steamboat on the river. You'll be sorry you ever come."

All morning and past noon we moved down the water, while the beauty of the river touched us with its spell, the long, graceful bends edged with emerald willows, the curving sand bars where flocks of stately white cranes stood motionless, like birds of ivory.

On the Arkansas shore smoke was arising. I saw that it drifted up from a mat plant, one of those vast industries of the army engineers charged with the maintenance of the channel. Here hundreds of Negroes were cutting the willows that grew along the bank; other black men wove them into immense carpets three hundred feet wide and sometimes a mile long. Near by a gang was lowering one of these enormous constructions into the water, to protect the levee from the river's currents.

Rhythmically the black men chanted as they labored:

> *Can't come to you, baby,*
> *Till that evening sun go down.*
> *Big old buzzard's in the sky,*
> *And a dead man's in the groun'.*

Near by were rows of tents and cabins where drab white women and gaudy-dressed Negresses sat gossiping, waiting until their men returned from their toil. A few hours later some of the tents would be crowded with somber figures bent over a deck of playing cards or a pair of rolling dice. There would be arguments, and fights, and perhaps a murder. These mat plants sheltered some queer characters. Like the levee camps, legend declared they were sanctuaries for any luckless fugitive from conscience or the law.

We tied up for a moment, and I chatted with a young, overalled Negro, come from some neighboring cotton field.

"They done killed a man here jest last week," he told me. "And a few days before that the police come to git a fellow robbed a bank in New Orleans. I don't want to kill or rob nobody. Unless maybe you could be like that man's the big robber over there in England across the ocean, the fellow they calls Red Riding Hood. He's the finest robber in the world, they says, takes the money from the rich folks and gives it to the poor. They got a million dollars reward out for him.

But they can't never catch him. He can run faster than a railroad train, they says. It's cause he's got quicksilver in his shoes."

Down the river we drifted again, past long sand bars and lonely lakes where floating ducks made rhythmic patterns on the glassy water. Great islands showed ahead, and chutes

that led off to some false channel, traps for the unwary voyager, where his craft might be held for months in the gluey river mud.

Big John steered warily.

We saw a towboat, grounded on a sand bar. Beside it a sister ship, with chains and lines, struggled to pull it free.

Big John swung us past a river light. "Everybody can make a mistake, except a pilot," he remarked with cynicism. "Bookkeeper can rub out his mistakes with a eraser. And a doctor can bury his. But a pilot puts his mistakes right out where everybody can see."

The sun began to set. We tied up for the night at the edge of a willowed island. The last line had barely been made fast when a thick fog swept over the river. The trees on the shore became gray shadows. As though the fog were some curious blotting paper slowly absorbing their substance, their trunks grew fainter and fainter, then finally vanished.

Night fell. The misty curtain grew denser. We could not see a foot beyond the windows; there were only waving layers of vapor. A deep silence fell over the river. I helped Big John cook our supper. We ate, speaking little. Occasionally from the near-by trees came the muffled cry of some marauding animal. Once from the mainland there drifted the mournful mooing of a cow.

There was a sudden sound of footsteps along the bank. Big John's eyes instinctively went to his rifle. We had thought the island deserted. We were approaching rough country; we could not be sure of any night-time visitor. There came a knock outside, startling in the stillness. I went to the door and saw an old white man whose wrinkled face was framed by a snowy beard and snowy hair. He spoke in a voice so low I could hardly hear. He was a shanty neighbor, who had seen us land, and had come to learn if he could borrow some coffee. I gave him some of our supply, and walked over to his dwelling. It was a pathetic shantyboat, neat, but almost barren of furniture. In a chair made of willow his wife was sitting, knitting a fishing net. Her hair, like his, was white with age; her face wrinkled, gentle.

They were a pious couple, going to a rustic church or a gathering of worshipers on some distant shanty whenever opportunity offered. They looked sadly upon their neighbors who drank or made moonshine liquor. Their proudest possession was a gift from some city dweller, a square of rainbow-colored glass, lettered in gold, and edged with a golden chain. Unable to read, they were nevertheless sure of its meaning; they knew it was one of those sacred mottoes, like GOD BLESS OUR HOME, which so often hung in the dwellings of their richer neighbors.

I read the sign to myself in all its rainbow glory. I did not tell them the meaning. The ornamented words were brief: DIXIE QUEEN BEER. THE BEST BEER IN THE VALLEY. PLEASE PAY WHEN SERVED.

I returned through the fog to our shanty, and went to bed.

All next day and the day after we glided down the stream, past towering pines and spreading cottonwoods and rows of stunted willows. The mouth of White River showed before us, whose waters years before had witnessed the great pearl rush for the treasures inside the lowly river mussels, with a city of ten thousand tents, and pearls worth sometimes three thousand dollars. Today there were only fishermen, and lumbermen, and gaunt moonshiners.

The country was flattening, with great swamps spread on every side. Long-legged cranes flew constantly over us; black-winged buzzards perched grimly on the shore, like frock-coated undertakers waiting for clients. Like the swamp birds, the shantyboats were increasing. Often in a sheltered cove we could see a grizzled shantyman tarring his fishing lines or drying the skin of some animal.

"Got to be careful of shanty people now," said Big John as we tied up for the night at the edge of a pine grove. "Most of 'ems finest people there is. But these swamps is mighty good for hiding. If I had the money you could get for catching all the fellows here the law's after, I'd be richer than a man I knowed once down in New Orleans was making counterfit money."

A rooster crowed on a shanty up the river. Big John listened intently.

"Haven't heard that bad news yet," I remarked. "That rooster saying anything special?"

Big John shook his head. "He's just doing ordinary crowing. That rooster up by Memphis was hollering plenty different. And plenty bad. You'll be finding out mighty quick."

The proprietor of the neighboring shanty came to call, a stout, genial fisherman, accompanied by two chunky little girls. I went out with him in a rowboat as he ran his lines. Once as we halted, a huge water moccasin, brown, hideous, crawled into the boat to steal part of the catch. The fat shantyman brushed it away with a stick, as casually as though the reptile had been a dried reed blown into the boat by a gust of wind.

Another rowboat drew up alongside, manned by a young-ish individual with a slippery, evil face and accents unlike the pleasant drawl of the river. He surveyed me in deep suspicion with narrow, bullet eyes, spoke to my fat host in mono-syllables, then rowed off beyond the trees.

"They says he killed a man in Texas," remarked my stout friend, amiably. "Used to be a band leader or something, they was telling me. I don't know. But he can sure play the harmonica. It's mighty nice when you got a fellow around can play music thataway."

He reached out to pick off a tiny measuring worm moving across my sleeve. He shook his head in warning. "You better be careful about letting them worms walk over you. They're trying to measure you for your graveclothes. If I hadn't got that one off before he walked all the way across, you'd be dead before the next full moon."

I went back to our boat, where Big John was busy cooking. It had been growing warmer all day. The air now was oppressive, stifling. The oppressiveness increased as darkness spread over the water. Lightning began to flash in the distant sky. We ate, and I went out with my companion to examine our moorings. A black roll of cloud was sweeping across the horizon, like a wide, smoking carpet.

Big John watched gloomily. "Worst part of the river for storms," he muttered. "Get a tornado quicker than a judge can say ten dollars. Tornadoes runs across here just like they was automobiles going on one of them big highways Hughie

Long built in Louisiana. Help me get a line around that stump. I want all the rope on this bank we can get."

We went inside, and making the shanty snug, sat waiting. The last of the stars overhead vanished. The tall pines to which we were moored were gloomily silhouetted against a

purplish-seething sky. Their tops began to sway a little. A faint staccato whistling began in the lower branches, like that of a frightened boy trying to keep up his courage in the dark. The lightning came nearer.

Suddenly there was a dull booming, like a distant explosion, coming nearer and nearer. The pressure in our ears changed sharply, as when one drops too swiftly in an elevator. The shanty was gripped in a roaring blackness. A flash of lightning cleft the sky. By its green glare we could see the water about us churned into great white-crested swells on which the shanty was bobbing wildly, like a float on the line of some colossal fisherman. An instant later rain began to fall in torrents. The din on the tin roof was loud as the roar of the steel mill from which the metal had come.

The lightning was continuous now, with the flashes coming in two directions, as though two rival societies were setting off immense firework bombs and rockets with a prize awarded for the most spectacular display. The beating of the rain and the boom of the thunder joined with the wind in a mad symphony. The tall pines swayed wildly to and fro, like crazed giants dancing in suicidal accompaniment. A tree crashed near us, and fell into the river, sending up a cataract of lightning-touched foam. The towering pine beside us bent and twisted in frenzy, as though it wished to follow.

We sat at the window watching the mooring lines that were our frail link to safety. Tighter and tighter they grew, like violin strings about to break. Suddenly we saw a curious movement in the line that ran from our stern to a tree. It was slowly twisting free.

With a bound Big John was out the door, and dashing across the slippery bank. I followed an instant after. The force of the wind was terrific. We could hardly stand. Half blinded by the lightning, I helped stretch a new line to a great log buried deep in the clay. We darted back to the shanty.

The roof was leaking badly. Rivulets of water poured everywhere from the ceiling. We put out pans to catch the overflow. The streams dripped musically onto the tins, in strange contrast with the clamor overhead.

The lightning began to grow paler. The deluge from the ceiling lessened until it became a series of single drops that struck the pans with a noise like a bell. The storm was over.

The last clouds, like whipped dogs, skulked off to the horizon. A crescent moon showed above the tops of the pines. The trees stood proudly erect again, like friendly sentinels. The pleasant smell of damp willows rose everywhere along the shore.

The air was fresh, invigorating, when we awakened in the morning. We took our accustomed places in the gasboat. We reached Yellow Bend, the dread of towboat captains bound upstream. We sped down it, the current so swift we had little need of our motor. Twice we passed towboats struggling to nose their barges up the racing water; with every pound of steam their boilers could hold without bursting they were able to advance only half a mile an hour. At the foot of the bend we saw three other large vessels, rearranging their convoys for that intricate operation known to towboatmen as double-tripping. In a difficult section of the river such as this, instead of taking its barges all together, the towboat would make two trips and sometimes three.

We stopped for eggs at a little farmhouse on the bank. We went into the chicken yard while a cheerful countrywoman, clad in a red house dress, searched in the straw near the clucking hens. A heavy pall of smoke lay over a near-by field.

"My brother Luke's burning it out to kill the snakes so we can raise some cotton," the red-clad matron remarked in explanation. "Bottoms here's just full of moccasins and rattlers."

Big John looked off thoughtfully where an overalled figure stood with a rake near the flames. "He better be mighty careful. When you burn a field that way all the snake poison goes into the smoke. You get just one puff of that smoke in your eyes, and you'll be stone blind the rest of your days."

The countrywoman nodded in agreement. "Luke's always careful about a snake. His father was bit by a snake. A rattler that had bit a copperhead. When a rattler bites a other kind of snake that way, he gets its poison, too. Double rattler, they calls it. The one bit Luke's father turned him blue as a jay-bird's tail. He ain't turned back to his natural color yet."

Toward dusk we saw the government fleet that marked Greenville, rich little metropolis of the Delta, and as darkness fell, came to rest at the foot of the levee. I wandered with Big John aimlessly through the town. Tonight the streets were crowded and the stores gay with neon lights of many colors. I remembered a visit when every light was dark and the streets were under many feet of water—the days of the great flood of 1927 when the levees protecting the city had broken. The river was so wide, I heard it said that preachers, called on to hold funeral services for the victims, were reading the ritual for those who died at sea; there was no land anywhere.

We returned to the shanty.

A towboat moved down the water with half a dozen barges,

its searchlight cutting a dazzling path through the blackness. The vessel turned toward the wharf. The wake struck us broadside. The shanty began to perform its usual frantic Dance of the Towboats. A dishpan leaped from its hook in the wall and went clanging to the floor. A huge wave splashed through the open window, covering our faces with a muddy spray.

The swells quieted.

I wiped my wet cheeks with a towel. "You'd think those pilots would slow down a little when they see a shantyboat," I remarked.

Big John's voice grew ominous. "Wait till we meet the *Sprague*," he said.

Day after day we proceeded, in a dreamy, never-ending world of swamps and swaying willows. Red birds flew like flaming arrows over white, deserted islands. Crows cawed mournfully as they drifted over brakes of tangled cane. Far across the levees, overalled black men and bandannaed women hoed their narrow fields of cotton; in a tiny village beyond, lazy rustics sat outside the general store, dozing torpidly in the sun. A clock ticked on a shelf of the shanty-boat. We looked at it rarely. Time, the harsh ruler of men in cities, had no force, no meaning, on the river.

We had left Arkansas behind. We were drifting between the shores of Mississippi and Louisiana. Spanish moss hung everywhere from the trees. Here and there we saw shantymen pulling the long strands from the branches, to await the visit of the mossboat. In some distant factory these fibers would be reborn as a mattress or a cushion for an automobile.

We were in the area of the great caving banks now. Often the shore would rise in a towering muddy cliff, seventy feet high, at whose bottom the river was gnawing greedily. As we drew near, Big John would steer far out into the river.

We would watch with fascination as some vast section of the clay wall collapsed with the roar of an avalanche into the river, carrying with it trees or river lights or any luckless cow that chanced to be grazing on the grass-covered top. I knew that the rules of the river were many for a shantyboat. But there was one rule above all others whose neglect meant certain tragedy. Always travel warily near a caving bank, and never, never anchor.

We stopped one afternoon to buy fish at a shantyboat, presided over by a tall, bony individual with keen, merry eyes. Quickly he introduced himself as Tooter Bill, and lifted out some catfish from a latticed trap in the water.

He slapped viciously at a mosquito on his arm. "Mosquitoes is bad this year," he drawled. "Was up at Jake Powers' farm yesterday up by Two Mile and the skeeters was so bad I seen his mules kick some flint stones laying there to make a spark and start a smudge fire in the grass, and then they stood in the smoke. Was all right I guess, till a bad wind got to blowing, and Jake got scared the fire'd catch the house. So he brought water from the river and put it out. The mules was mighty sore."

A dilapidated dog, which had been trailing at the shantyman's heels, bounded suddenly off into the brush.

"After a fox, I reckon," drawled Tooter. "Never catch him though. Foxes round here are the smartest there is. There's one fox lives off a little ways with his pardner. And all they do is think up ways to torment that poor dog. While ago they done like what they call them potato races at the County Fair. One fox'd run my dog awhile, and when that fox got tired, he'd come back and let the second fox take a turn doing it. Kept it up all day. Then when they didn't want to run no more, they sat up and licked their paws to kill the scent, so the dog couldn't follow. I seen foxes doing that plenty of times. When the dog come back, for a month pretty near he walked like he was one of them dogs they used to have in front of the rich people's houses in Vicksburg. He was made of stone."

We sputtered down the river. A series of new muddy cliffs rose before us. Thick foam, like the suds floating in a tub after a heavy washing, appeared here and there on the surface of the water.

Big John studied them closely. "Banks is caving plenty today," he announced. "When you see foam that way it's a mighty sure sign."

A sudden fog swept over the valley. In an instant the shore was blotted from view. Big John slackened our pace to a crawl.

Strange foggy shapes began to drift before us, great whitish masses, at times like rows of high-domed Arab mosques, at times like ranges of snow-covered mountains. Long streamers of mist followed, like the pennants of some advancing ghostly army. After them came spectral whales and ships with full sails flyings. A real ship showed ahead, a steamboat, with its running lights glowing faintly. It bore down on us with no slackening of its speed. To its pilot we were only another phantom of the mist. Big John raced the engine and swung the rudder. I clicked an electric torch as a signal. The light was dim. We did not know whether its rays could reach the steersman at the far-off wheel.

Nearer and nearer the shadowy hulk swept toward us. We

could hear the troubled sighing of the smokestacks. Then a bell in the engine room tinkled musically. There came the swish of reversing paddles. The onrush of the vessel grew slower and slower. It turned away, missing us by what seemed the thickness of one of the heavy ropes coiled at the bow.

We went on slowly again through the mist. Some branches marking the shore appeared ahead. We halted, rejoicing in our haven, like travelers in a storm suddenly come upon a cozy inn. We had remained only a few moments when there came a terrific roar behind us, and the sound of a chaotic splashing. In the mist we had anchored beside a caving bank. New roars followed at irregular intervals. Stones and earth began to rattle upon the shanty roof. Big John raced the engine once more; soon we were in open water.

My companion's tense face relaxed. "Sure a quiet life on the river," he said.

Next day Vicksburg showed ahead, high on the bluffs where the Confederate cannon so long had held off the besieging soldiers of the North. Up the hilly roads we climbed, beneath the moss-covered live oaks that shaded the pillared houses. On the main street, thronged with gay-dressed black men and women, a mountain of fried catfish showed in a store window; near by a stately Negress in the white robes of a nun preached to a black, intent circle on the virtues of a new religion.

We continued our journey. Natchez appeared around a bend, looking down like a haughty Southern belle on rustic

Vidalia, slumbering in the bottom lands that formed the opposite shore. We pushed on steadily. We were in the heart of the Mississippi swamps. Immense buzzards perched everywhere on the branches of the drowning cypresses, and moccasins coiled on rotting logs; occasionally when we halted we caught a glimpse of an alligator crawling clumsily over the mud until it vanished in the tangled brush. Always when we camped at night there were queer noises in the trees. Often we could see pairs of tiny green eyes, a fox, or possum, or perhaps a wildcat.

Now and then the men and women who dwelt along the river shores had caught the bleak contagion of the landscape. They were silent, melancholy, like the gloomy cypresses.

We stopped at the shantyboat of an old Negro, anchored beside a river light. "You ain't got no stomach medicine, have you, Captain?" he asked us anxiously. "I was gitting along fine till I come in here, and now I got stomach pains all the time. I kind of figure maybe somebody's a-poisoning me."

He pointed off to the bank. "I got that light I takes care of for the government, and two more round the bend. They gives me ten dollars apiece for doing it, that's thirty dollars a month. That's a heap of money. There's plenty of people around here'd like to git them lights away from me. Couple of times there was holes chopped in the bottom of my gasboat, so when I was just a little way out the water come in, and I pretty near drowned. Way my stomach's a-hurting, looks to me sure like somebody's trying to kill me to git that thirty dollars."

We gave him some medicine, and went on, wondering.

Dismal Swamp showed before us, and the country beyond where legend declared the land lay under a curse, and all the inhabitants, white and black, came to some appalling end.

Here, Negroes said, in the olden days on a rich plantation, offending slaves had been tied to high wagon wheels and rolled to their deaths in the river. On stormy nights their ghosts, still bound to the huge wooden circles, could be seen rolling over the swamps, crying out to any passer-by for mercy.

Past Old River we glided, the mournful country of the

great overflows; past Angola, with its grim blockhouses, where the guards of the penitentiary stood with their rifles; past Baton Rouge, with its lofty State Capitol towering into the sky.

The landscape changed violently. The swamps, the sand bars, vanished. We were traveling between two immense levees that rose on either side like the walls of some mighty fortress. Beyond the embankments were fields of sugar cane, and cheerful Cajun villages, where the jovial inhabitants gossiped in excited accents over their cups of violent French coffee.

We stopped at Donaldsonville, resting peacefully in the bayous, and chugged onward. We were nearing the end of our voyage. When we moored for the night at the foot of a levee, New Orleans was only fifty miles away.

"That bad news has got to come pretty quick if it's coming," I told Big John, with optimism.

He munched his tobacco ominously. "We ain't got there yet," he grunted.

A genial, bearded trapper lived with his wife in a shanty beached a short distance up the levee. We paid a brief visit to learn if we could purchase some corn. I noticed a gay little raccoon on the shanty porch, slapping playfully at an old bulldog dozing in a corner.

The trapper, smoking a corncob pipe, gazed at the little animal with deep affection. "Smartest coon you ever seen," he declared. "Steals my pipe, and then brings it back to me with the black stuff all cleaned out and the bowl all polished up, till it shines like the looking glasses in them saloons down in New Orleans. Likes beer, too. Drinks a bottle without stopping. The bulldog's the same way."

He glanced off toward his wife, busy with her cooking, and winked at me broadly. "Every Saturday night, when the old woman ain't looking, the coon and the dog and me goes out and gets us some beer. And we all get drunk together."

We sauntered back to our moorings.

We went to sleep with the sound of a distant church bell ringing in our ears.

I awakened suddenly, to find Big John shaking me vigorously by the arm.

I sat bolt upright and glanced out at the moonlit water.

A giant towboat was coming down the river, pushing a score of shadowy barges. Even in the distance I could sense the vessel's immensity. A deep, musical whistle echoed between the levees.

"Better get up," urged the figure beside me. "Big Mama's coming. It's the *Sprague*."

I pulled on trousers and my shoes.

The monstrous steamboat continued to swing down the river.

A small tug lay above us, laboriously pushing three barges of sand up the current. The thunderous whistle of the *Sprague* blew again, in signal. The tug answered, feebly.

Suddenly there came from the smaller craft's trio of barges

a strange clanking sound, as of a series of metallic explosions. The barges leaped apart and began to drift down the stream.

"She's broke up the tow," grunted Big John. "We'll get it in a minute."

He dashed onto the shanty deck. I followed quickly. The tug began a frantic attempt to rescue its charges.

The giant steamboat bore down on us, her searchlight piercing the night like the tail of a racing comet. As she swept past I could see that her enormous paddle wheel made other wheels on the Mississippi appear like the work of Pygmies. It seemed the wheel of the peerless *Huronoco*, that mythical queen of all good steamboats whose exploits pilots tell to their cubs on the long watches of the river nights. From the huge wooden blades was falling a vast Niagara.

Suddenly the shanty rose in the air as though struck by some strange underwater earthquake. The two lines that held us to the shore parted as if they were rotted threads. Black mountains of water assailed us. The shanty seemed to stand on end, then lay heavily on its side. Great muddy seas swept over the deck. Streams of water poured from our hair and clothing, as though we were sponges just lifted from a bath. Another swell struck, flinging the wooden hull fiercely against the bank. Blow after blow followed, as though the vessel were in the grip of some furious water monster, bent on its destruction. The frail boards seemed ready to crack with each repeated onslaught. Each new shock seemed about to inflict the mortal wound that would send us to the bottom.

The waves lessened. The shanty began to flounder drunk-
enly down the current. Quickly Big John caught up the
steering pole and brought it to the land.

We made fast once more, and drenched to the skin, went
inside the shanty. The floor was covered **with water**, rapidly

seeping through the joints of the planking. In the murky
liquid lay every pot and pan that had hung on the wall in
our trim kitchen, and the shattered remains of the china with
the bluish cows which had been Big John's pride.

We took brooms and swept the watery floor.

Big John surveyed the broken china with gloomy eyes.
"That Memphis fellow you rented the shanty from sure's

going to be mad," he told me. "Them cows was the prettiest china I ever seen. The cups and saucers cost fifteen cents apiece, the fellow told me. And the little bowls was a quarter and the big bowls was fifty. I bet you there's four dollars a-laying there in pieces on the floor."

We tied up next afternoon at New Orleans, halting a few miles from the center of the town to avoid the crowded harbor. All about us a myriad water craft were hurrying, ferryboats and steamboats and long tows of barges, tugboats and lighters and rusty ocean freighters, on their way to the Gulf and the drowsy seas beyond. Over the levee came the honking of auto horns, and the dull rumble that marked a great city.

I settled my debt with Big John, who was to take the shanty off to a near-by canal to await its owner. He helped pile my suitcases into the car of a friend, and bidding me good-by, started back toward the river.

He halted, and slowly retraced his steps. "About that rooster," he said. "I been thinking. I guess he was hollering to you about what happened to them dishes. Five dollars is a heap of dishes to be breaking. If it wasn't them dishes, it's something still a-coming. You be careful in New Orleans. It's a mighty bad town."

He climbed aboard the gasboat and started the engine. The shanty vanished into the smoky horizon.

SHOWBOATMAN

Crown the buzzard and crown the crow
She's all loaded up and blowin' to go
                                    —RIVER SONG

SHOWBOATMAN

I

You can see him any day, standing on the deck of the *Goldenrod* at St. Louis, smoking a thick cigar and looking out at the muddy Mississippi. A heavy-set, genial figure, with a smile that a candidate for President would envy, he does not appear to be a man who in a week often had more adventures than most have in a lifetime, and who for nearly fifty years made theatrical and river history; who owned seventeen famous showboats and steamboats, and now owns the last showboat left on the river.

He is Captain Bill Menke, king of Mississippi showboat-men.

"I guess only a crazy man would run a showboat," says Captain Bill. "It's a great life. But it's like being in the Fun

House out at an amusement park. You never know when the floor's coming up to slap you down."

Take an old frame church such as can be seen in any small American town, remove the steeple and press down the roof so that the whole building flattens out a little, cover it with white icing so that it looks like something between an ivory cuckoo clock and one of those frosted Easter eggs with a little window at one end, set the whole affair on a huge barge with a steamboat behind to push it over the water, and you have a good idea of the *Goldenrod* or any old-time Mississippi showboat.

At the bow as the visitor comes up the gangplank is the little ticket office, from which strategic post, as though it were the bridge of a great ocean liner, Captain Bill directs the activities of the whole floating enterprise. Beyond is a long, two-storied auditorium, much resembling the interior of the village Opera House once so common throughout rustic America. The scenery behind the footlights is likewise of the sort so familiar to every small-town theatergoer of thirty or forty years ago; when the heavy roller curtain descends, it falls with a noise like thunder. The stage and the whole theater list a trifle as is proper in a building of such mellowness and antiquity.

Here every night, winter and summer, Captain Bill's actors tramp the boards, some young hopefuls just embarking on their footlight careers, some battle-scarred veterans of carnivals and tent shows, who for a long time have shared Captain

Bill's tribulations and triumphs. Here they perform their old-time melodramas that portray the perils of heroines like that of *The Moonshiner's Daughter,* or recount the tearful tragedy of *Nellie, The Beautiful Cloak Model.* From St. Louis and all over the United States visitors come to see this remnant of the old Mississippi that has somehow survived into the mechanized, high-pressure life of today. Each week end this last of the showboat queens is filled with a crowd many a New York theater would envy.

At eight o'clock on a typical Saturday night the automobiles draw up on the *Goldenrod* wharf, the drivers cursing occasionally as they dodge the giant mooring rings set for the steamboats in the slippery cobblestones. The visitors straggle aboard, and take their places on the creaky seats inside. There is a flurry of activity behind the curtain, and a noise of last-minute shifting of scenery. Soon a fine-featured, dignified woman with slightly graying hair comes into the orchestra pit, and sitting down at a battered piano, begins to play an overture. The music ends, and the curtain rises. The pianist goes off to play the part of an ailing grandmother, and the show is on.

In harsh whispers the black-cloaked villain, hiding behind the paint-peeling trees, plots the destruction of the hero and his loving family. And with each move of every actor, the audience hastens to come to their assistance. If the villain is preparing a new lure for his victim, the audience shouts a warning; if the erring hero falls at the feet of his beautiful wife to beg her forgiveness, the audience, too, implores her to pardon his sin.

Twenty years ago, in the small towns of the Mississippi Valley, Captain Bill was presenting these melodramas with no thought of burlesque. So seriously were they regarded by the river audience, that once up the Monongahela, when the cast was playing *Uncle Tom's Cabin*, a wild-eyed coal miner dashed onto the stage, and brandishing a pistol, demanded that Legree stop horsewhipping the patient old slave or pay for his cruelty with his life. There are still remote areas of the Mississippi where a similar incident could be repeated today.

I sat with Captain Bill in his office as he listened to the loud-speaker connected with the theater, so that he could hear the dialogue of the actors and the banter of the audience.

His usually genial face grew troubled. He arose from his chair. "Getting too noisy," he declared. "Have to quiet 'em down a little. Crowds are funny. Easy for 'em to get out of control."

He came back in a few moments, smiling. "Have to be a diplomat on a showboat. I've had to handle everything from a dancing girl to a devilfish twenty-five feet wide. That's what keeps me young."

Few stories are more colorful than a simple recounting of Captain Bill's life. Born in Cincinnati, where the green hills come rolling down to the Ohio, even when a small boy he knew that the wanderlust was in his blood.

But there was no chance to realize his longing until the age of twenty-one, when a railroad friend gave him a pass to ride a caboose to New Jersey, where his brother Ben was working in a large watch factory. As the young voyager looked out of the caboose window at the passing towns and fields, he knew that he would never be happy except with a life of travel and adventure. He joined his brother at the workbench fashioning timepieces, but his heart lay elsewhere. All his leisure hours he spent at the water front of near-by Hoboken, watching the rusty freighters and the stately liners glide out to sea. The youthful watchmaker knew nothing of sailing or watercraft; nevertheless he decided he must have a boat of his own. Joined by his brother, he constructed a little vessel thirty-six feet long, calling it the *Cincy* in honor of his home town. As ignorant of piloting as a cowhand in Texas, he quit his job in the factory, and began to operate the craft as an excursion boat for sight-seers around New York Harbor.

But salt water was not to the liking of this native of a river town. He decided to take the vessel home and show it to the folks. With his brother, he put the craft on a freight car, and sliding it into the muddy Ohio at Pittsburgh, floated down between the smoky hills to Cincinnati.

It was at the Ohio metropolis that Bill's fertile mind conceived a new plan. The showboats moving up and down the river had always captured his imagination; his cherished ambition was to be a showboat owner. Now he took steps to make his dream actuality. The latest invention of the day, the motion picture, was making its first feeble appearances here and there around the country. The young Cincinnatian secured a shabby picture machine and five worn-out films, including *The Great Train Robbery* and *The Sinking of the Maine*. Adding to this equipment one of his mother's best bed sheets as a curtain, and a huge can of oatmeal as the main food supply, on New Year's Day, 1905, Bill set out with his brother in their little homemade vessel to conquer the Ohio and the world. The great Menke showboat was a tolerable success for a few weeks. Each night they stopped in a different settlement, playing in a schoolroom or a vacant store; enough of the townspeople came to see their scratchy offering to keep some bread and occasional meat on the table.

But suddenly one of those intense cold waves for which the region is noted swept down through the Valley, freezing the river solid. The boat, halting for a show at Uniontown, Kentucky, was caught in the ice as effectively as though trapped at the North Pole. Bill and his brother set up their machine in an unoccupied building. A few came for the first performance. But Uniontown was a one-night stand. On the nights that followed, the seats were empty. Week after week, the young impresarios lived in their icebound craft, helpless, shivering. The money with which they had started was long since spent; all their food supplies except the oatmeal had vanished. Three times a day they ate nothing but the gluey cereal. They had begun by liking oatmeal. Now they regarded it as a special kind of poison. Often in the middle of the night, Bill would wake up freezing, sore with hunger, and cook more oatmeal on the tiny stove. Ben, his brother, would give a groan, and join in his grim repast.

For a time matters appeared to improve. There came a thaw, and the embryo showmen hastily moved on to a new precarious stand. But the ice closed in again; the situation was worse than ever. Then one night at a ferry landing alongside, they found a crateful of eggs, probably forgotten by some bottom farmer. They had not eaten an egg for months, and taking a couple of dozen back to the boat, celebrated with an egg orgy. But after Bill had gone to bed, he began to have twinges of conscience. After all, taking two dozen eggs was no different than taking the money some buyer would have paid in a grocery store. Bill spent a considerable part of the night arguing with his troubled soul. As he lay awake he heard dogs barking now and then near the ferry. Early in the morning he went to shore, to find the owner and make restitution. And then to his joy, as he neared the crate, he saw there was nothing left inside but a mass of broken shells and a thin yellow paste which some flea-bitten hounds were licking hungrily. The neighborhood dogs had come in the darkness and ruined the whole lot. There was no need of worrying any longer. The dogs had covered up the hungry brothers' tracks, and wiped out their crime. The eggs would have all been spoiled anyway. The moral of which story, says Captain Bill with a twinkle in his eye, is that man's best friend is always the dog.

The ice broke soon after, freeing the imprisoned show-men, and their boat continued on its way. But there was little improvement in their finances.

Then a miracle occurred. Down the water came the huge showboat, French's *New Sensation,* famous everywhere along the Western Rivers. By a lucky chance the captain needed

two advance men, the professional name for the billposters who went through the country a week or two ahead of the vessel, putting up the bills that announced its coming. The starving young adventurers and their little boat got the job.

To be a billposter, a vital part of a real showboat's activity, was more than Bill had even dared hope. It was backbreaking work in those days. Generally Bill would go on foot, carrying his paste buckets far back into the country; sometimes he would hire a rickety wagon, and jolting all day over the stony creek bottoms, return late at night, weary and supperless. But no billposter ever pasted up his daubs with more enthusiasm.

"I've walked all the way from the head of the Mississippi to the Gulf putting up posters," Captain Bill will remark as you stroll about with him, inspecting the showboat. "I'll bet there isn't a barn or a board fence I've missed unless it's been built since."

Oddly enough, there was something in the paste to the particular liking of farm animals. Many times Captain Bill would put up his posters on a barn, only to pass by a little later and see half a dozen cows licking off the last scraps of his gaudy broadsides.

Every few weeks it was necessary for Bill to return to the *New Sensation* for instructions. Here he saw at close hand the glamorous life that combined the romance of the theater and the river; the parades with the band decked out in their scarlet and gold uniforms; the deep-voiced actors that walked up and down the boat like rival kings; the beautiful actresses who occasionally would reward the young advance man for some service with a smile. Here he heard the quavering notes of the calliope echoing over the water, unlike any other music in the world. He determined more than ever that someday he would manage his own showboat.

It was a long, difficult struggle, a constant saving of every penny. Most of the time he continued to work as billposter on one of the showboats touring the Valley; when the river jobs ended with the season he took any employment he could find on the shore.

At last in the spring of 1911 came the historic day when Bill had put aside enough money to buy an interest in a showboat, the *Sunny South*. With pride, as the calliope began to peal out its musical thunder, he looked at the little town where his newly acquired treasure was to make its first landing. Dazedly he put on the captain's dress uniform of glittering green and silver, so hot that almost instantly perspiration dripped into his shoes; taking his place at the head of the band, where the waiting drummers and cornetists were playing like mad, he gave a signal, and led the parade up the wharf. Bill's youthful dream had come true.

It was a dream full of comedy—and nightmare. Show business in any form is erratic, plunging in a moment from the height of success to dismal failure. On the showboat another factor was added even more unpredictable than the show—the river.

The new venture had been proceeding pleasantly enough for a few months, and the *Sunny South* was playing the drowsy little towns in the bayous of the Evangeline country, when near Franklin, Louisiana, the catastrophe fell that was every riverman's unspoken horror in the days of wooden hulls. The boat hit a snag hidden under the surface and tore a great hole in the speeding prow. The river began to pour through the break like a muddy cataract. In a few moments the vessel would sink to the bottom. Captain Bill gave a single glance at the wound threatening the prize for which he had so long labored, then took the action that will keep his name famous among rivermen as long as a paddle wheel churns the Mississippi. Snatching some bedclothes from his cabin, Captain Bill dashed back to the streaming bow, and wrapping the comforters and blankets around him, jumped feet first into the hole. His plump body, with the addition of the bedclothes, fitted to perfection. There he remained as a human cork for almost two hours, his legs dangling beneath the hull, till the carpenter could arrange a more permanent plug, and the shattered boat was watertight once more.

"I'll never live that one down if I get to be two hundred," says Captain Bill. "Somebody told me they even wrote a song about it. But I don't believe it's so."

For several years life for Captain Bill proceeded in the usual fashion of showboatmen. Sometimes the boat's attraction was an old-time melodrama, *Way Down East* or *Ten Nights in a Barroom,* or some current theatrical success of the day. More often the program was vaudeville and variety.

The show would open with a group of gay-clad chorus girls, dancing and singing in the fashion typical of the time; they would be followed perhaps by a juggler or a stately Swiss bell ringer. After this a Valley Houdini might emerge handcuffed from a water barrel, or the Mario Brothers would shout vain commands at their troop of monkeys, racing madly on roller skates. Then the Dainty Sisters would trip lightly from the the wings and whirl fans or Indian clubs as they danced across a swaying wire; they might be followed by a robust comedy, *Why Men Leave Home*.

A brief intermission would occur with the Oleo, where members of the cast, doubling from some earlier appearance, would perform some specialty act, a black-faced tap dance or a sentimental song. Then the regular show proceeded once more, with a magician who produced a pigeon out of a child's pocket, followed perhaps by an artist who made portraits of the Presidents out of dishrags, or an athletic young woman wearing white tights who posed as statues of ancient Greece and Rome. After this long preparation would come the headline act of the show, *Creation*, where a pretty girl swung on a great steel arm over the audience and appeared to emerge from a budding flower; or Fearnot, who climbed a ladder to the top of the stage, and dived into a tank of flaming oil. A moment later all the cast would join in the grand finale, immediately followed by a one-reel motion picture, a travelogue such as *The Johnstown Flood* or a current comedy. Then the audience would go up the bank and drive off in their lantern-lit wagons, to talk about the thrilling events of the night until the next year.

Generally the boat followed the seasonal moods of the patrons—and the crops. Captain Bill's route was a calendar of the resources of the Mississippi Valley. In the early spring he would go up the Monongahela, visiting the coal miners; then in the summer, he would slowly voyage down the Ohio and up the Mississippi, following the harvests of wheat and corn. Late in the fall he would start for the South where the inhabitants of the plantation settlements were preparing to pick and gin their cotton, then tour in the winter around New Orleans and the bayous for the workers in the rice mills and the fields of sugar cane.

Then one unhappy day a chance visitor told Captain Bill of the rich region that lay along the Alabama and Warrior rivers above Mobile and its historic bay. The area was virgin territory for showboats, said the newcomer, and its fertile bottom lands grew so many bales of cotton to the acre, even the smallest tenant farmer lived like a king; if Captain Bill could get the *Sunny South* up into those waters, overnight he would become a millionaire.

Captain Bill believed the glib stranger and prepared for the expedition to the Promised Land.

"I get sick even now when I think of what that fellow did to me," says Captain Bill, shaking his head ruefully.

To reach Mobile from the Mississippi requires a lengthy trip in the open expanse of the Gulf of Mexico. The excursion was an almost suicidal test for Captain Bill's wooden-hulled river boat; unsuited for rough water, with the slightest swell it was apt to break in two. To make matters worse, as the vessel neared salt water, the pilots were all ocean steersmen, ignorant of the ways of the Mississippi.

A pilot came aboard at the danger point, a cocky little man who took the wheel as casually as though he were steering a child's tricycle. When Captain Bill's questions showed his concern, the cocky little man's expression became one of hurt dignity. "What's so different with a river boat?" he asked.

They started out without too much trouble, and had traveled in the open Gulf for perhaps half a mile, when a violent wind arose without warning; the boat began to leap and sway giddily. Even on a river, showboats were always difficult to maneuver; to cursing pilots they were known as balloons or windcastles because their great height caught each trace of breeze like a sail. For an hour the steersman tried to navigate the vessel across the ever-shifting waves; with each new tack it spun more dizzily. At last Captain Bill took the wheel and brought it into port himself.

Four more times the pilot set out, and four more times Captain Bill brought the boat back to where she had started. Two weeks passed while they waited for a day when the troubled waters would be quiet. Then a morning dawned with a thick fog that reduced visibility to zero.

"Now's the time to cross," said the cocky little man. "She'll be smooth as asphalt with this fog all over."

They were out for only ten minutes when Captain Bill knew they were hopelessly lost. Great rocks would loom suddenly a few feet before the bow; now and then the gray shape of an ocean boat would take form in the mist, and charge toward them like an angry ghost. The pilot would swing the wheel frantically, missing the other craft by inches. Then the waves began again, soon becoming the deadly, pounding swells of the Gulf, that seem the size of mountains.

The boat began to leak in half a dozen places. Captain Bill put every pump to working, but it had no effect on the streaming torrents in the hold. The wind increased and the water grew deeper. Again and again as a great wave struck,

there would come an explosive cracking of timbers, and the boat seemed about to break apart. The actors gathered in a circle on the stage, and dropping to their knees, began to pray.

"If you wanted to hear some fancy language spoken to the Almighty, you should have heard those actors," declares Captain Bill.

Somehow the vessel reached Mobile, and made its way up the Alabama River. And there the Promised Land proved only a new series of trials. The cotton crop was a failure that year, and the rich farmers of whom they had heard had enough difficulty finding their turnip greens and corn bread, without worrying over the problem of paying fifty cents to a showboat.

"It was terrible," says Captain Bill. "Even the chickens and the turkeys were so skinny, you felt too sorry for 'em to eat 'em. One night we gave a benefit performance for the poor people of Selma, Alabama. We should have given the benefit for ourselves. We were poorer than anybody there."

But worst of all was the matter of the airplane. Before starting, Captain Bill at great expense had obtained a hydroplane and a stunt pilot, thinking that in the year 1914 when an airman was a novelty in the area, he would give a free exhibition and bring people to visit the showboat. The sightseers came as he planned; sometimes five thousand farmers were gathered on the riverbank. But half of the spectators were too excited by the plane's flying to care to see a theatrical exhibition afterward. The other half said the whole thing was a trick, that the plane wasn't really flying at all, and they wouldn't come on any boat run by such a big faker.

Typical of this latter attitude was a tobacco-munching farmer who stood near Captain Bill on the shore one afternoon, watching as the airman climbed into the craft, and tuned the engine for his flight.

The farmer spat a cud of tobacco. "It ain't a-going to fly," he announced solemnly.

A few moments later the plane rose up from the water.

"Ain't a-going to fly very high," prophesied the rustic.

Just at that instant the airman circled, and soared into the clouds.

The farmer turned to go down the bank. "Well, anyway, it can't carry no freight," he declared.

"I guess I was just ahead of my time," says Captain Bill.

Months afterward the travelers crossed the Gulf again, dead broke, with the *Sunny South* looking as if it had been wrecked in battle. They had scarcely reached the Mississippi, when Captain Bill was greeted with the news that the bank had foreclosed, and the boat was lost to him forever.

Captain Bill went back to billposting again, and started his life all over.

For two years he labored, skimping every penny. Then in 1917, joined by his other two brothers, Harry and Charley, he bought another showboat, the *Greater New York*. They owned her five days when she sank in a devastating windstorm, uninsured, a total loss. This tragedy, coming so close to his earlier misfortune, would have ended the career of many a less sturdy character. But Captain Bill comes of the breed of men who are indestructible. The storm had sunk a steamboat near by belonging to a towing company; divers said it could never be raised. Captain Bill and his brothers bought the wreck for a song, and erecting a tent along the bank, began to try their own salvage operations. All summer they worked, borrowing pumps and hoses from a neighboring factory, patching day and night; when autumn came the steamboat was once more afloat and ready for new voyages. A big grain contractor chanced to come along at the moment who needed a boat to haul his heavy purchases of corn. Captain Bill undertook the task with the resurrected vessel; when the season ended, he had earned enough to buy another showboat, the famous *New Sensation,* for which he had posted bills many years before.

II

From that time on Captain Bill's career may be called fairly stable, if there can be said to be any stability in show business. He never left the showboats again. But it was a career that would have made a nervous wreck of a man of conventional mentality. The fragile vessels were always getting smashed up in the ice or being crushed by drifting barges; Captain Bill would buy a new one, and sometimes two. Once in Illinois at a time when he owned a pair of showboats, at the very instant one was gliding down the bank from the dry dock where it had been repaired after being almost destroyed in a tornado, a new storm wrecked her twin lower down the river. Next day she was towed up to the same dry dock to take the place of her mended sister on the ways.

Yet so careful a riverman was Captain Bill, that in spite of his eighteen showboats and steamboats and their thousands of miles of traveling, not a passenger was ever involved in even a minor accident.

Captain Bill took pains to see that the hours of the visitors on one of his craft were peaceful. For himself and the cast and the crew, life was a series of daily emergencies. In unknown territory brushes with the law were regular as the sunrise.

One day the boat lay along the Illinois shore of the Ohio, in the heart of the region known as Little Egypt. A large crowd had come aboard and the show was just ready to begin, when a rough individual wearing a sheriff's badge tramped on deck, followed by two ugly-looking deputies.

"We don't allow no shows here on Sunday," barked the officer. "Give all them people their money back and tell 'em to get off the boat."

Captain Bill looked at the packed theater, and his ruddy face turned gray. Business had been at the vanishing point and this was his first chance in weeks to recoup his losses; now the rich opportunity must be tossed away. He thought quickly what might be done to retrieve the catastrophe. And then he remembered something he had learned from his years of travel on the river.

Ordering the mate to pull up the gangplank so the showboat would no longer be connected with the shore, he turned to the belligerent visitor.

"Got a ticket to get on this boat?" Captain Bill demanded.

"I don't need no ticket. I'm the sheriff," the other grumbled.

"You're not the sheriff where you are now," Captain Bill told him. "You're an Illinois sheriff, and we're in Kentucky. The Kentucky line runs to the water's edge here, and you know that as well as I do. Sunday shows aren't against the law around this part of Kentucky. You buy a ticket or get off my boat."

The sheriff left in a hurry, for he knew Captain Bill was right. The showman kept the gangplank raised till the performance was over, and then let it fall, and everybody went ashore. The receipts that day broke the record for months.

But perhaps Captain Bill's funniest encounter with the law was on the ill-starred trip to Alabama. The boat had landed at one of those little towns where the local officials were noted for their expertness in collecting petty graft. In the cast at the time was a young actor named Jack, who liked to spend his leisure hours fishing.

Late in the afternoon Jack was out on the stern, trying to catch a catfish for his supper, when a deputy sheriff came striding up the gangplank, one of those lanky rustics the actors called swamp angels, with hair so long it was supposed to grow through the top of their weather-beaten hats. The newcomer demanded to know if Jack possessed a license, and on being informed to the contrary, nodded with satisfaction.

"You're under arrest," he grunted. "Round here you don't do no fishing unless you got a license. You come on up town right now to the jail. We got to teach you smart actor fellows a lesson."

Again Captain Bill was compelled to do some agile thinking. The show was beginning in a little while, and Jack played an important part; he might be lost for hours in a hopeless encounter with a justice of the peace. Captain Bill managed to get a quiet word to the beleaguered actor; an instant later Jack made an excuse to go off to his room. When he returned, he was no longer the same person. He went in a young man, wearing a gay-colored shirt and checked trousers, for he bore the reputation of the boat's sportiest dresser. When he walked out, he was an old man with a shabby black suit and a beard. The deputy searched the boat for several hours—but he couldn't find his fisherman anywhere.

"We stayed in the town a week after that," relates Captain Bill. "And a couple of other times Jack thought the deputy suspected, so he changed his costume again. It wasn't really necessary. But Jack was an actor. And you know how actors are."

Other crises were constantly arising. Some of the river towns were full of bad characters, and moonshine was cheap and plentiful. Many times Captain Bill stood on the gangplank with a pistol, facing a crowd of drunken bullies threatening to rush on board and break up the show. On occasions there would be a religious group that objected bitterly to the boat's coming, as the consummation of evil and sin. More than once the vessel was moored near the tent of an evangelist or a church of the Holy Rollers, where far into the night the crew could hear themselves denounced by a swaying, chanting crowd as emissaries of the devil. Captain Bill never knew when the worshipers' frenzy might cause them to snatch up clubs and axes, and reduce the showboat to a gaudy ruin.

The feature of the showboat best known to residents of the Mississippi Valley **was the calliope.** There are few hamlets

on a navigable river of the region which have not at some time heard one of Captain Bill's boats burst into a concert of steamy melodies.

I was sitting with him at the railing of the *Goldenrod* on a quiet afternoon, when a passing towboat chanced to blow for a landing, a squat Diesel with a flat, unmusical whistle.

Captain Bill's genial face showed his disapproval. "They

could use some of my old calliopes on these new boats. That was real river music, the calliope. The best ads in the world, too. You could hear 'em for eight miles."

The towboat blew another flat blast. Captain Bill winced again. "I'd have rather lost almost anything than a good calliope or a good calliope player. Not one in a hundred pianists could ever learn how to handle 'em. You needed fingers strong as a blacksmith because of the steam pressure. The best players on the river were Crazy Frank and a girl they called Louisville Lou."

There is a strange story of Captain Bill and a calliope. The showboat was playing in a little town on Bayou Teche, not many miles from New Orleans. A woman was in the local jail waiting to be hanged, the only one of her sex, according to reports, ever sentenced to execution in Louisiana. The showboat was at the settlement for some time, and each afternoon entertained the residents with a program of songs on the calliope. One day the condemned woman sent word to Captain Bill to say how much she enjoyed the playing, and would he please play something while she was being hung.

"I did what she asked," said Captain Bill. "Human beings are hard to figure out sometimes."

He lit a black cigar. "I remember another time we played the calliope. It was on the upper Mississippi, and we were passing the state penitentiary where they said the man that wrote the *Prisoner's Song* was behind the bars. We played the *Prisoner's Song* on the calliope when we passed, and people around there said it made him mighty happy. We never played it after that. The *Prisoner's Song* and *Home Sweet Home* are bad luck on a showboat."

He noticed my smile and grew serious. "All right. I know you think I'm foolish. But I'll tell you something that happened right in your home town of Covington. We were playing down at the foot of Russell Street there, doing wonderful business, when a new calliope player came on the boat from a circus, didn't know about showboats, and before I could stop him he played *Home Sweet Home* all the way through. Half an hour later something went wrong with the government dam at Fernbank and all the water rushed out. We came down like an elevator, right on a snag that ripped a big hole in her bottom. It took all summer before we got her raised."

A serious problem with the calliope was keeping it repaired. Out in the open night and day, exposed to every kind of weather, the keys were always sticking and rusting, making the playing of certain notes impossible. Moreover, the whistles were easy to remove. Often some knowing tramp living on the riverbank would come aboard at an unguarded moment and carry off one of the metal tubes to a junk yard, where he would trade it for the price of a whisky.

Parades were another feature of showboat life familiar to every Mississippi dweller. With his cast and crew, Captain Bill sometimes employed as many as sixty people on the showboat and the steamboat which was its motive power. When they paraded through a town in their rainbow uniforms, he strung out the marchers so expertly that with the help of a dozen town boys properly costumed for the occasion, the procession appeared to number at least two hundred. On occasion, when some notable in a settlement died, Captain Bill would tactfully lend the showboat band to join in the funeral. With proper melancholy they would proceed to the cemetery, playing the solemn strains of the *Dead March,* then gaily return to take up their places as the showboat orchestra.

It needed a many-sided individual to be a showboat captain. He had to be at once pilot, caterer, doctor, diver. He had to be a tremendous gambler, gambling with that most unpredictable of all things, public taste.

He had to decide whether the moment was ripe for a guillotine act, where a man seems to chop off a woman's head, or whether it was chorus girls who might be demanded; he had to decide whether to choose a husband who sawed his wife in half, or ladies dressed like butterflies who swung from wires by their teeth.

Even with the best of acts something was always happening to upset his calculations. There was never a day when he could be certain of the outcome. A good show town without reason would suddenly become calamitous; a bad one overnight would become a triumph. One dismal afternoon in an autumn downpour, the showboat halted at the tiny settlement of Gold Dust, Tennessee, not far above Memphis. The only place for the landing was far from the roadway. Access

to the boat was impossible except for a walk of several hundred yards through knee-deep mud. Captain Bill looked at the
dripping skies and was sure every seat would be empty. To
his amazement, at six o'clock, two hours before the performance, the bank was lined with the country people of the
region, who had not seen a show for years. Hungry for entertainment, they were not to be cheated of their opportunity.
Men and women of every age took off their shoes and stock-
ings, and wading through the mud to the boat, packed it to
the railing.

The picturesque characters who have walked the decks of
Captain Bill's boats in half a century are innumerable. Famous among his staff at St. Louis today is Bruley, the cook,
who joined Captain Bill forty years ago as a female imperson-
ator in the days when that type of entertainment was usual,
and weary of acting, ended by taking charge of the ship's
galley. Bruley emerged as the vessel's savior once in the depths
of Arkansas. The show of the moment had a leading lady,
very comely and popular; but she had neglected to tell Captain
Bill that she possessed a husband who objected violently to
her theatrical career. One night after the performance, the
furious spouse appeared on the bank with a pistol, two burly
assistants, and a waiting automobile. While a single deck hand
looked on dumfounded, he whisked her into the car and
vanished up the river. Captain Bill had no understudies; with
his star performer gone, the situation seemed hopeless. It was
then that Bruley, back in the kitchen, hurried to the rescue.

It had not been long since he had ceased his female imper-
sonations. His make-up was still handy; he was sure he could
learn the lines in a hurry. For two months he played the part
of the kidnaped beauty, while his pots and pans rusted in the
kitchen.

"He was a great success," relates Captain Bill. "Nobody
ever knew the difference. But everybody was kicking about
the food, and I was glad when he went back to his dishes. It's
easier to get a good actor than a good cook."

The performers were often a problem. It was a favorite trick
years ago for impecunious actors, not careful of professional
ethics, to advertise in a theatrical magazine, and when the
notice was answered and transportation funds forwarded,
never to appear but to spend the money instead paying their
board bill. There was one actor Captain Bill had never seen
who had played this trick upon the showman, and extracted
forty dollars at a moment·when his failure to arrive was particularly troublesome.

Captain Bill had never forgotten. "I'll fix that fellow if it
takes a lifetime," he told himself, and waited for the day of
Judgment.

It came two years later on the upper Ohio, when Captain
Bill chanced to see in another advertisement that his ancient
enemy was making his headquarters in the sleepy little town
where the boat had just landed. The showman warmed with
the thought of his vengeance.

Hurrying off to the address, he found a shabby hotel, and

making inquiry of the clerk, climbed up four flights of dingy stairs. In a freezing room, he found a white-haired old actor, half starved and lying ill in bed with pneumonia.

"Instead of getting my money back, I felt so sorry for him I sent him off to the hospital," says Captain Bill ruefully. "Before I was through with him it cost me a hundred dollars."

The animals on the Menke showboats were always as individual as the actors. One of the most popular members of the staff was the captain's rooster, known as Mike. A handsome Rhode Island Red, Mike was a Casanova celebrated among hens far and wide along the Mississippi. Whenever opportunity offered he would go to the town where the boat had landed, pick a fight with some local feathered cavalier, and start back up the gangplank, proudly escorting two or three of the most prized members of his victim's harem. On more than one occasion when business was bad and food supplies were of the scantiest, it was Mike that kept the larder supplied with chicken.

It was among the steamboat crew, always noted for eccentricity, that the most peculiar characters under Captain Bill's banner were to be discovered. There was an engineer who afraid of being attacked in his cabin, booby-trapped it with rows of tomato cans on strings, so that any intruder would trip and set off the alarm; he also arranged little nooses of twine to catch rats in the same ingenious fashion. There was the deck hand at St. Louis, who when not working on the boat, slept each night in the near-by park, but always drove to the park in a taxi. Towering above all was Tom Garrison, the pilot. Tom was a stout figure, of the size and girth of William Howard Taft. Much of his pay was spent on his clothes; always he went about in an expensive black suit, with a broad

black hat to match, and two gold watches and two gold chains, the repetition being intended to double the effect of the whole impressive costume.

"Everybody that looked at Tom thought he was a governor or a U.S. Senator," said Captain Bill chuckling, as we sat watching a tug on the river while it struggled to move a government dredge over to the Illinois shore. "Tom always carried some buckshot in his mouth, and he could spit em out as accurately as a rifle. He'd pick some ugly-looking customer eating supper in a hotel dining room, and drop a shot in his soup a good thirty feet away. Of course the fellow eating would get wild and accuse somebody else of doing it. A couple of times some terrific fights started. But nobody'd think of suspecting Tom. He was a real card."

On one occasion Captain Bill put the pilot's talents to good use. They were traveling up the Tennessee River, and the Tennessee bridges were notoriously slow in opening to let the steamboats pass; the rivermen declared the rustic bridge tenders were too busy making moonshine when the whistles blew, and didn't want to spoil the run. It was Tom's first trip, and he was unknown in the area. Whenever the showboat neared a slow bridge, Captain Bill would bring it to the bank. The stately pilot would pay a solemn call on the bridgekeeper, and in his most magisterial tones, say that he had come from the War Department in Washington because of the many complaints. He would further inform the cowed bridgeman how this interference with navigation was a federal crime which might jail the offender for the rest of his natural life. For a long time after that visit the Tennessee bridges were said to be the fastest opening anywhere.

But what Captain Bill enjoyed more than anything else was his fight with Captain Ralph Emerson, who owned the largest showboat on the Mississippi.

"It was a knock-down and drag-out fight," said Captain Bill, chewing his cigar reminiscently. "No holds barred. If his advance men came to a town where my billposters had already been busy, he'd cover up all my paper, and what he couldn't cover he'd tear down. And you can bet I'd do the same whenever I had the chance. Maybe I wouldn't have fought him so hard if his boat hadn't been bigger than all the others, and he never let us forget it. His showboat carried a banner: YOU'VE SEEN THE MINNOWS. NOW SEE THE WHALE. That got under my skin."

Constantly the rivals struggled to be first in a new territory, for the first to arrive always secured the cream of the trade. Knowing that Emerson was watching every move, Captain Bill would often try to send him on a false scent, billing a poor show town when he had no idea of playing it, hoping that Emerson would swallow the bait and go there himself, leaving Captain Bill to exploit some richer field. At times he would go so far as to actually make a landing at the less desirable community, but would take care to sell no tickets. Quietly he would wait there until Emerson followed and had taken on a few customers so that his boat could not move away. Captain Bill would then steam off to the good show town and play to a large audience. The contest grew so intense that once at Hannibal, Missouri, the rival boats were struggling at the same moment for the only good mooring. Captain Bill won it, with Emerson racing so furiously behind he stove in his bow on the bank.

Yet the two men were good friends, with the greatest admiration for each other. Every New Year's they would spend three days together, staying at the same hotel, calling on old show friends, and conducting themselves like brothers. When the three days were up, they would separate and fight like tigers all the rest of the year.

Captain Bill's greatest triumph over his rival occurred in their battle for the Monongahela, always known as the best showboat territory on the Western Rivers. The coal miners were eager for a show after being shut up all winter, and more than anywhere else, the first showboat to arrive was always a sellout. The coal workers would come down to the river in boxcars and flatcars if snow made the ground impassable. If there was no boat landing, they would build one in a day with slag from the mines.

"It was early spring," said Captain Bill, chuckling again. "I had the boat in dry dock up on the Ohio, getting some pretty big repairs we needed before we could make our Monongahela tour, when one day Ralph Emerson happened to come to town. He was so tickled when he saw my boat laid up he couldn't talk hardly. But he tried to look sympathetic.

'Too bad, Bill,' he said. 'Way they've got you in the hospital here you won't even get started for the Monongahela before two months, I guess, will you?'

'Two and a half's more like it,' I answered.

"He nodded, and I could see he was almost choking, he was so happy. 'Well, I'm mighty sorry for you, Bill. I'll be up there in three weeks anyway. Looks like it's going to be a fine year. I'll give 'em all your regards.'

"Well, that was too much for me. As soon as he was gone I got hold of the owner of the dry docks.

'How long did you say it would be before my boat's ready?' I asked him.

'Six weeks. Not a day sooner,' he said.

'I want her out in a week,' I told him. 'Hire every boatbuilder on the Western Rivers if you have to. I don't care how much it costs. But get her in the water.'

"He thought I'd lost my mind, but he did what I asked him. He hired men from all around there, everybody who'd ever been near a boat yard. I steamed up to the Monongahela as fast as I could go, and made a fortune. A couple of weeks later Emerson came along. You can imagine what he said when he found out I'd been there first."

Captain Bill tapped the railing where we were sitting. His blue eyes twinkled brightly. "This was his boat, the *Goldenrod*, the biggest showboat ever built on the Mississippi. I bought it from him when he gave up the river. We're the best of friends now, all the time. I see him every year."

We went inside to Captain Bill's little office, hung with pictures of notables who have been visitors. Captain Bill, at seventy, is a national institution.

A towboat went up the river, pushing a score of tank barges loaded with oil from Texas. The *Goldenrod* began to rock heavily in its wake.

The towboat whistled, a long, deep call that echoed in melancholy over the water.

Captain Bill listened, then picked up a pile of letters and telegrams wrapped with a rubber band on his desk.

His face glowed with youthful enthusiasm. "Next year I think I'll start traveling again. I've got enough offers and guarantees here to pack the boat every night for a couple of seasons. Gertrude Lawrence says she'll come whenever I'm ready. And there are a lot of others. I've got a new steel hull, twenty-eight compartments, so we can go anywhere. The *Goldenrod's* had a wonderful life, and she's still got a long life ahead of her."

It's the same way with Captain Bill.

EAST MEETS WEST

Catfish dance and shantymen fiddle,
Sing me a song and I'll tell you a riddle.
Eko, Iko, where are you going?
I'm going where there's trees and the tall grass growing
—Fiddle Tune

EAST MEETS WEST

THEIR names are Dip Gee, Ping Wing, George Lum, and Ah Hee. They live in strange wooden villages built on stilts far out at sea. The voyager in a boat, looking at these queer structures with their Oriental occupants, would be certain he was passing some exotic settlement near Shanghai or Hong Kong or Singapore. Actually he would be in Barataria Bay, that ragged arm of the Gulf of Mexico which reaches up into Louisiana, only a few scant miles from New Orleans. The Chinese would be the owners of the shrimp platforms near Manila Village, in the great marshes that lie at the mouth of the Mississippi.

It is a place of mystery, this region of the marshes, a half-world that is neither land nor water, of giant reeds and green floating islands that dissolve into the sea. Overhead the great man-of-war birds fly in stately circles, and the porpoise that the fisherfolk say are really men dance and play in the sunlight. The fleecy clouds that drift across the sky become camels and graceful sailing ships and all the shapes of fantasy. It is a land like the Sahara, where the horizon seems to enclose only a world of mirages, and all life seems to be moving in a dream.

It is a background appropriate to the shrimp platforms, for even as the traveler comes closer to inspect them in detail the sense of illusion continues, the feeling that these tiny buildings and the figures moving about them are something conjured out of the sleeve of an Oriental magician.

For they are a perfect stage-set, with their netted shrimp boats moored alongside, like a trading post in some Pacific archipelago. They are stage-sets populated by a group of actors of extraordinary variety, of men who come from every quarter of the globe with no questions asked as to their history—a Foreign Legion of the Mississippi. They are one more manifestation of that amazing phenomenon that is America.

The platforms are, in effect, large wooden islands—several acres of buildings and boardwalks, with a store and sheds and numerous tiny dwellings to house the motley inhabitants. Their trade is a considerable part of the vast Louisiana commerce in shrimp, which has totaled half the shrimp commerce of the nation. Yet the whole industry of the platforms has sprung from an oddity of appetite—a peculiarity of the Oriental palate. The Westerner, in eating shrimp, likes them either canned or fresh; the Oriental is not satisfied unless his shrimp are dried.

It is natural, then, that the most prominent feature of these structures is the row of drying platforms, long, narrow elevations built in waves, like a series of roller coasters. Here workers take the shrimp from huge kettles of boiling brine, and place them at the top of the wooden hills so that any water will drain quickly away. For days the shrimp lie in the burning sun, protected if it rains, by wide tarpaulins. When the last drop of moisture has vanished they go off to the shelling machines, revolving drums with long spikes inside, like medieval instruments of torture. Soon the shells are broken away and crushed into powder. The shrimp are packed into barrels and made ready for a long journey. Weeks later they will appear in a Chinese restaurant in New York or South America or far-off Honolulu. The casual Broadwayite with his steaming chow mein or the Hawaiian with his shrimp and pineapple, will eat and have no slightest thought of his meal's strange origin.

A walk about one of the platforms is a tour around the world; their languages are as numerous as the Tower of Babel. "Manuelo!" calls a woman's voice, and there climbs down from a boat a Spaniard with a costume so flamboyant he might have stepped from a scene in *Carmen.* "You no catch shrimp today, Kin?" asks a tall Slavic figure as he passes a Filipino walking with a pretty little wife and toddling baby. Sewing up a net is a Portuguese, dark as ebony, whose accents mark him from the Cabinda, steaming African colony at the mouth of the Congo; in the doorway of a tin-roofed hut there stands a brawny Turk. Once there was even a Laplander, named appropriately, Iceport. There are many Cajuns, genial souls speaking the rough French patois of the marshes, with an occasional American from Texas or Montana or the hills of Arkansas; adventurers all, come to try their luck at the shrimp, the leaping gold of the sea. Over them presides the Chinese proprietor, like Mr. Wing of Ping and Wing, who sits each day in his little store at Manila Village, seeing all, knowing all, yet always remaining bland, courteous, imperturbable.

Just how the platforms started there seems to be some question. Information about the marshes is often as hazy as the gray fog that rolls in from the horizon. Some say that a China-man was the first builder, who came in the adventurous Eighties from Canton. The most authentic legend seems to be that Manila Village was founded by a Filipino who chanced to visit the area, an alert traveler named Kin Ting. The waters of Barataria Bay and the Gulf beyond teemed with shrimp, so prized by the Oriental taste. Why not, thought Kin, start a colony of fishermen to catch and prepare shrimp for the Oriental market?

The idea, once born, was quickly put into execution. Other Orientals came to join the pioneer. Out of the shallow bay rose the little wooden huts of the fishermen, on stilts as they had been built for centuries in Kin's native land. Despite the mosquitoes that swept out from the reeds in steamy masses, so thick they resembled a cloud, the village grew and prospered. Soon two hundred fishermen, mostly Filipinos, moored their boats at the tiny wharves. Regularly they gathered as the shrimp were brought from the boiling kettles and piled on the platform in great slippery mounds; with heavy-booted feet they tramped away the shells, as the peasants of Europe tramped their grapes for wine. Dried shrimp from Manila Village began to go out to China and the world. As Kin prospered, others followed his example, now employing fishermen of all nationalities; in a short time seven shrimp platforms dotted the waters of the bay. It has been many years since Kin's men drove the first pile below the muddy water. But his memory lingers. To this day all Filipinos at Manila Village are nicknamed Kin.

There are still two hundred fishermen living on each of the platforms in the season, rough individuals in close quarters, with an atmosphere much like that of the old sailing ships in the days when the pirate Lafitte was ruler of the marshes. Like all humanity they vary, the good and the bad. They are subject to all the strains and emotions common to undisciplined men who live together as they labor. Sometimes, particularly on Saturday night, when the rougher ones have drunk heavily, a fight may start with the suddenness of a bomb, and the bland proprietor must interfere to keep the battle from spreading. Yet the lack of violent crime among them is remarkable.

Children of Noah

This is probably due to the childish simplicity of most of the inhabitants; they possess a kindliness that many of the dwellers on the mainland might envy.

A friend of mine was engaged in rescue work among some of these shrimp fishermen during the great hurricane that struck the region in 1947. For a number of days the rescue workers had been trying to reach one group completely isolated by the huge tidal seas, and certain that all their food had been washed away, were greatly concerned that they might be starving.

After a tremendous struggle, the rescuers at last reached the battered dock, with its buildings still under two feet of water. As they feared, they found the fishermen gathered in a half-submerged shed, exhausted and suffering acutely from hunger. As the rescuers hastened to distribute their supplies, my friend noticed half a dozen great fish swimming about in the water that covered the floor, washed into the building at the height of the storm, and trapped in some fashion so they could not escape. So helpless they could have been caught by a child, they would have provided an excellent meal for all those marooned in the shed's narrow quarters.

My friend, wondering, asked why the shrimpers didn't eat the fish, instead of almost starving.

The fisherman he addressed, a gaunt Mississippian, looked at him in shocked surprise. "We couldn't eat them fish," he answered. "Them fish were fighting for their lives, same as us."

Today the men on the platforms come and go freely, as men go anywhere. There have been times, not many years ago, at the height of the shrimping season, when shanghai parties would hurry off to shore, and gather up all the wrecks of humanity that lay numb with drink in the dives of New Orleans. This practice increased the infinite variety of the platforms' population. One might be a doctor, another a bank clerk, one a broken-down actor, another a roving iron worker; all the usual flotsam and jetsam of the Boweries of the world, "on the skids" from trouble or alcohol. Some of these derelicts, benefited by the hardy life and the fresh sea breezes, elected to stay on the platforms, and working for good pay, were restored to society. Others, wearying of raising nets or minding the boiling kettles, left for the mainland and their old dives once more.

There were rumors in the past on certain platforms of other breaches of the law. There were stories of immigrants being smuggled into the marshes from some remote harbor of Cuba or Mexico, grim tales of Chinamen fastened to chains; when in a pursuit the chain was tossed overboard, Chinamen and evidence went swiftly to the bottom. There were rumors of dope, and of marijuana growing in flowerpots before a fisherman's door. At times a government boat would steam up to the wharf, and the white-clad officers would search diligently. But in later years the owners of the platforms have been watchful of their tenants, and the coastguardsmen no longer keep such a wary eye.

It is a man's world, the platforms, though there are some women. Often a more serious fisherman, a Filipino or a Cajun, will bring a wife from shore. There have been many fine children brought up on the platforms, their schooling perhaps sketchy, but their minds keen in the ways of the porpoise and the pelican. With all the races and nations represented, the result of the marriages is often unpredictable, the more extraordinary products being jocularly known by the name of the complex distillation of sea food so popular in the region, a "Gumbo Filé."

In this half-world of the marshes, where a distant cloud becomes a green island of rushes, and an island with trees and passing sailboats proves only a cloud, it is easy for even the sophisticated to credit the weird and the magical. Small wonder, then, that superstition is widespread among the fishermen, particularly those older individuals, who unable to read or write, are unaware of scientific discovery. If a woman chances to step on a fisherman's gear, all fishing for the day might as well be abandoned. Never a shrimp will come into his net, and even the lowliest garfish will scorn his most succulent baiting. If he should stamp on the great Congo snake that hides out in the steamy marshes, he is certain to be afflicted with a violent attack of rheumatism. If he is troubled with those odd sinus headaches known to the fishermen always as "sun-pains," there is an easy remedy. He has only to hear of an old woman in the marshes gifted as a healer, and reach her cabin before the break of day. When he tells her his name and the date of his birth, she will make a cross on his forehead, and blow the pain away.

The sky, the earth, are full of signs and portents. Even the cats who stalk haughtily up and down the platforms, fat

as prize pigs on endless banquets of shrimp, are regarded by some of the veteran fishermen as possessing special power.

"I tell you, my friend, this is so," said Henrique, a little old Cajun with wrinkled, leathery face that matched the bare feet he was dangling over the side of his shrimp boat. "Maybe you think is crazy but these cats they can tell the hurricane. Ten years ago there is a cat here named Lobito, belong to a Portuguese we call Jo. This cat Lobito, when the wind going to blow, his fur get sticky like molasses, and he not eat shrimp or nothing. Only he sit and cry, like a baby when the milk in the stomach turn to gas. And in his eyes, which are green, come many white spots, like you sprinkle sugar, maybe. It is by a cat's eyes that you tell the weather, my friend. This time the spots in Lobito's eyes are the worst I have seen. Big like rice when my wife cook it good in Lafitte. I tell you when I see this, I am very afraid. I tell the other fisherman. 'There is going to be one terrible storm,' I say. 'Tie your boat with many ropes, and tie it with the anchor. Maybe it is better if you go far away from here, up the Mississippi.'

"Some of the fishermen listen to me, and look at the cat and say 'O.K., Henrique,' and tie their ropes. Some laugh and say 'Henrique, you big fool'—but they tie the ropes anyway. That night the hurricane come, the worst hurricane ever Barataria. It kill plenty people all over. But here nobody. It was this cat which save them, everyone."

He made an expert cigarette of the tobacco I had brought him. "The cats they maybe needed not so much now, maybe. The men of the Coast Guard and the radio they watch these big storm and tell the people. But ask me, my friend, and I will tell you. Between the radio and a cat like this Lobito, I will take the cat."

There is good reason to fear the hurricanes. Of the seven platforms that once flourished, only four remain; the three others lie at the bottom of the bay, crumpled by the wind and the water.

Characters like Henrique seem to develop on the platforms as easily as the tall grass grows in the marshes; others are attracted, as though by some natural force, like gravity. Each new shrimp boat that ties up alongside may add a new picturesque resident. There was one platform dweller, nicknamed Cock-a-Doodle, who went about his daily rounds strutting like a chicken, and who when asked a question was apt to answer by crowing like a rooster.

There was one man said to be a duke, and another an ex-millionaire; there were others, more mysterious, fled to the marshes for safety from the law. At intervals, even today, a state or federal boat comes up to one of the platforms to disembark a detective. There are a few quiet inquiries, and some stranger, lately come to the region, is taken away in handcuffs, leaving his fellows to speculate for weeks whether love of woman or money was the reason for his fall.

But perhaps most remarkable of all the picturesque inhabitants was dapper Theophile, of Paris, a devotee of fine food and grand opera, who though he worked as a laborer on the platforms, legend said belonged to the highest social world of the French metropolis. Six months of each year, rumor reported, he spent in grimy overalls, his companions the pungent shrimp; the other six months he spent in a Tuxedo with the perfumed queens of French society, working as a gigolo.

There have been characters among the proprietors of the platforms as well, generally Orientals, though now and then an American has been owner of one of the properties. There was one fat Chinese, who waddled about with Chinese servants padding before and behind, like some august Oriental emperor. There was another owner, in sharp contrast, who everywhere he went practiced expert feats of sleight of hand, for the entertainment of all he encountered.

There is universal admiration for these Chinese proprietors among the fishermen and the dwellers on the shore. They never cheat, say those with whom they deal, they never forget a favor. An American I know chanced to do a slight courtesy for two of these Chinese who together operated one of the platforms. Years later the American set up his own business. On the same day, within a few hours of each other, both the Chinamen came to pay a friendly call, and each offered to lend him twenty-five thousand dollars.

To be a successful platform operator a man, whatever his nationality, must know when to see nothing and know when to interfere. Above all he must possess the tact of a saint. The shrimpers, like most fishermen, are notoriously prodigal of their money. With their childish natures, they will spend the earnings of weeks on some useless trifle pressed on them by a clever salesman as a gift for a wife or a new-found girl on the shore. At the end of the year, though pay in a good season is high, the most improvident often owe a considerable sum to the proprietor. But that tactful individual, in figuring the accounts, always takes care never to report the disastrous truth, and sees that a little cash is forthcoming. For like a child who receives nothing when all the other children are laden with presents, the fisherman would sit about and sulk; next morning he would steal off in a boat going to the shore and be lost to the platform forever.

The shrimper does not stay constantly on his wooden island. When the nets begin to come up empty and the trapping season is right, many of the fishermen take to the near-by marshes, to catch the muskrat and the other furry animals that roam the grassy wastes. Up and down the limpid bayous they paddle their pirogues, often cutting a new channel across the swamp to reach some distant trapping ground. Here in tiny cabins they live alone for weeks, with only the mewing of the white sea gulls and the cry of the loon for company. They may work for a time helping the Frenchmen up a bayou; they may call on the fresh-water fishermen who live in their shantyboats up Bayou Pigeon and Sorel, catching the catfish and the buffalo.

"I tell you, my friend, after you work on the platform you get along good in the marsh with everybody," said the wrinkled Henrique, as he calked a seam in his battered boat. "Only do not come in a pirogue where Jean Lafitte bury all his money. Somebody cut your throat quick. This is what a Sabine of the Indian people has told me, and it is they who know where this money is buried. There been plenty Indian people work on the platforms. Plenty people say they French or Spanish, when they are Indian. I tell you sure, my friend, how to find out if a man have this Indian blood. Make him to write something on a piece of paper. If he is even one small part Indian, somewhere in the writing he will put a little arrow. Indian people cannot write without putting in an arrow."

As the fisherman roams about this mysterious wilderness, he may meet a startling visitor, a strange-looking vehicle that can move over grass or water—the marsh-buggy of an oil company searching for a site to drill a well. And he will regard it with deep suspicion as a dweller in the open, the Arab in his desert, the Westerner on his prairie, always regards the approach of the newcomer that threatens his domain. For oil has wrought vast changes in the marshes, and the fishermen say, is driving both the fish and the animals away. Derricks rise everywhere and drilling crews churn the waters that once knew only the turtle or the alligator. Machinery clanks and groans behind some trapper's cabin, and the great pumps labor miles out in the Gulf. At night the flares leap luridly into the sky.

The fisherman will wander for weeks along the bayous, even stop for a while in some little town. But if he is a true son of the platforms, when the shrimp are running again he will return to his queer wooden village, to buy his tobacco from the bland, imperturbable Chinaman, and join the fleet of great-netted boats circling near the horizon. He may grow old and die on the platform, to be buried in the "Chinese graveyard" that lies at the extremity, one of those curious stonelike piles so common in the region, where the water has swept up the oyster shells and formed a shallow island. Here he sleeps with his old boat mates, washed by the waves that gave him his life.

Or if with age he can work no more and must leave the platform, he will not move far away. He will go only to Lafitte, sleepy, pleasant village at the edge of the mainland, where he can buy his groceries at the friendly store run by his old employer who once owned the platform at Manila Village. Sitting about with his comrades, he can talk of the hurricanes, and the Saturday nights when the catch was big, and Frenchie, the accordionist, drank his red wine and played like the angels in heaven.

For they ask little, these men of the platforms and the marshes, Frenchman or Greek, Yugoslav or Turk, Texan or hillbilly from Arkansas. They are dreamers all, who live under the magic spell of the river and the sea.

Their attitude toward life is perhaps best expressed by Captain Frank, the weather-beaten philosopher who lives alone at the end of the marshes, on a boat where the shrimpers and the other fishing craft must stop as they enter Louisiana waters. Holding no college degrees, Captain Frank has studied the plants and animals of the region with an intentness and an expertness that have won him the admiration of the state's men of science. Here beside a stretch of marsh which most call Devil's Island, Captain Frank, by himself occasionally for two hundred days at a time, has found some of the answers to the riddle of the universe.

"How can any person be lonely in the marshes?" he asks, while a great brown gull, who is one of his pets, stands on a piling near the boat waiting patiently for a scrap from the kitchen. "If he wants music, there is always the sound of the waves. If he wants pictures, there are always the clouds, going past all day, like a circus parade. There are the otters that make chute-the-chutes out of mud and slide down them like children. There are the porpoise that dance, and the birds on their way north or south, their wings every color of the sunset. There is God's great gift to us, the bird, though some people don't recognize their blessings. I'd sooner kill a man than kill a bird."

He took out his worn diary, and showed me the entry of the previous afternoon: *Today there were worlds of cormorants and one friendly loon.* "Lonely? There is so much going on it would take a man with a thousand eyes and ears to watch or hear properly. Awhile ago I saw a small plant on one of the islands here suddenly begin to shake and twitch, though there wasn't a trace of wind blowing. I searched carefully and couldn't find any animal in the branches, or anything alive in the ground about the roots. Yet the plant kept moving. What's the answer? I'm still puzzled. Maybe there's some tiny animal or worm inside shifting its weight. Or maybe there's some life in vegetation that we haven't yet learned about. Here I can worry over the problem. On shore it's always money, money, money. Out here in the marshes we don't worry about money."

The gull on the piling flapped its wings as a delicate hint that it was still waiting. Captain Frank tossed it a bit of fish, and called to some other gulls standing off at a distance, as a farm woman calls her chickens. His weather-beaten face lighted as they came flocking. "It's like this about money. It's what an old Indian I met out here told me. God made paper money, and it blows away. God made silver money, and it rolls away. If God had wanted you to keep money, he'd have made it square like dice so it would stay where you put it."

The birds ate, then flew away to follow a boat bound for one of the distant shrimp platforms. White, motionless they floated, sometimes appearing like magic creatures carved from ivory, sometimes seeming to dissolve and become part of the fleecy clouds drifting across the sky in all the shapes of fantasy. Below them the porpoise that the fisherfolk say are really men danced and played in the blue water.

It is a place of mystery, the marshes—and of wisdom.

HEADWATERS OF THE CUMBERLAND

Big Stone Gap is a getting mighty cold.
The hills is for the poor man, the cities is for gold
—STRINGY BOB'S SONG

THE KENTUCKY MOUNTAINEER

Dark, mysterious, the great Appalachian ridge known as Pine Mountain rises from the green Cumberland Valley, stretching out endlessly to the horizon, as though it were a Chinese wall built to keep all those who dwell behind it in a world apart.

The wall is breaking. The life behind the lofty ridge is changing. Automobiles roll down the passes where once only a mule could wander, and the juke box bellows in the little towns that once knew only the mountain fiddler. But so much of the spirit of the old life, so many of the old ways remain, the Kentucky Cumberlands and the neighboring peaks and valleys are still a region without parallel in America.

For here as in a museum the vast changes that have come in the world are clearly visible, changes of a hundred years that have sometimes taken place in ten; here often the traveler can see the life of our day marching hand in hand with the eighteenth century.

It is in the towns where most of the changes have occurred, with their schools, and stores, and filling stations, which look much like those of any other settlement of the lowlands. It is in the towns where the contrasts are most evident. The owner of a modern store who goes each year to a Rotary convention in Chicago or Los Angeles, may sell some groceries to an old woman who swears that a neighbor has bewitched her only cow. Some conflict between the new and the old is always occurring. In a little town I visited, a mountaineer, looking in vain for a place to tie his horse, hitched the animal to one of the parking meters just installed before the courthouse. Arrested by an overzealous officer, he showed how he had paid his nickel, just as any auto driver; a keen-witted old man, with the native intelligence for which so many of the mountaineers are noted, he argued that the parking space was for all kinds of transportation, whether it used gas or hay. The judge agreed, and horseman and horse went back home in triumph.

At the edge of the towns, however, the pavement ends abruptly. Let the traveler take a horse, or a jeep, or his own good legs, and go up one of the creeks or branches that wind between the towering hills; in a few miles he is in another universe. He will see cabins where the mountaineer who heads the family, if necessary can live almost as free of the outside world as his pioneer ancestors who came from Virginia in their rumbling wagons. He will find old women who, if the need arose, could take out a dust-covered spinning wheel from the storeroom, and make their clothing from the wool of the sheep grazing in the valley. Now and then he will find a poor cabin where those within have no lamp or candle, only a torch made from pitch pine.

Except perhaps for the Mississippi fisherman on his shantyboat, there is no one in all America as self-sufficient as the Kentucky mountaineer. Self-sufficiency was necessary in the earlier days if he was not to perish; after many years of isolation, he has become the most independent man in the world.

This independence is the mainspring of the mountaineer's existence, which determines every action of his life. He will receive the most casual stranger with a hospitality unbelievable to one who knows only the ways of the cities, sharing without a thought his last crust of corn bread; he will accept with stoicism any trial that stern Nature sends upon him and his fields. But let his freedom be threatened and he is instantly revolutionized. The quietness, the gentleness, become blazing anger; the lamb becomes a raging lion.

It was this spirit in the past which caused so many of the feud tragedies. The mountaineer's house was his castle and the lands about it his unchallenged domain. Let anyone invade either, and the intruder's life was the penalty. The early surveyors were often in a hurry and the surveys sketchy. Disputes over boundaries were thus inevitable. The ensuing feuds were wars between rival kings.

It was this independent spirit again, that in so many areas gave rise to moonshining. Corn was the only crop the mountaineer could plant on the rocky slopes that rose abruptly from the twisting creeks. Without highways or railroads, he could not send that corn to compete with the crops of the abundant lowlands. The only way he could ship his harvest was to turn it into liquid freight—whisky. It was his corn, he argued to himself; thus it was his liquor, his legal property. Anyone who interfered, such as a revenue officer, was acting in illegal fashion. Therefore it was as lawful to shoot the revenuer as to shoot a man trying to steal his timber or his cow.

Moonshining is practiced today by a small minority. But the attitude toward it in some areas is so casual, now and then there are complications. At a mountain school I know, maintained by one of the churches, and deeply opposed to any form of liquor, the lady principal was surprised one morning to find a sweet-faced little girl standing outside the porch. A paper scrawled by a neighbor and pinned to her dress, explained that the newcomer was being sent by her grandfather so that she might learn to read and write, advantages of which he himself had been deprived. The note went on to say the grandfather lacked the few scant dollars which each new student was expected to bring as nominal tuition; instead he was leaving one of the products of his farm which he hoped would be enough to satisfy the required fee. The principal looked at the burlap-covered box beside the girl, and opening it, found several gallons of moonshine whisky. There was a hurried conference of the faculty; soon a decision was made, with the tact teachers find so necessary in the mountains. The principal accepted the new pupil; then under the protection of darkness, poured the tuition fee into the creek.

The hunger for learning of the moonshining grandfather is typical of all his mountain fellows. Because of their long isolation, most of the older men and women are illiterate. But on every occasion they seek with pathetic eagerness for knowledge of the world beyond their mountain wall.

Once on a walking trip with my wife, we chanced to stop at a cabin where a bright-eyed old man was sitting, resting from his labors in the cornfield beyond. He made us welcome, plying us with questions about the great cities that lay along the rivers and the distant sea. In our talking he learned that my wife was a Canadian, whose ancestors had come from England in the days of the early settlement of the Dominion.

His shining eyes grew brighter. He studied my wife's face a moment, and taking her hand, held it warmly. "I've always wanted to meet a Briton," he declared. "All my life I've wanted to meet a Briton."

For an hour we talked; then it was time for us to go.

The old man took my wife's hand again. His face grew wistful. "When you git back to Canada," he said, "I'd mighty like it if you'd git all your kinfolk lined up in a row, and take a picture of 'em, and then write their names and addresses underneath and send 'em to me. I'd mighty like to git in correspondence with 'em."

The mountain schools are the centers where old and young alike learn something of this outer world beyond the misty horizon. There is a naturalness about the best of these mountain institutions that many a university with a vast endowment might envy. I have met the dean of a mountain college who goes out several times a year with scissors and clippers to cut the hair of an aged neighbor unable to afford the services of the barber in the town. The young students have a radiance in their faces quite unknown to the residents of the cities; it is eloquent testimony to what our mechanized civilization, despite its advantages, has lost.

The churches of the area, like the schools, are unpretentious. The native religion has suffered little change. The traveler in some remote region may still come upon a foot washing, conducted with biblical simplicity; he may still chance to see a funeralizing, always startling to any but the natives.

The funeralizing is a service for the dead. But it is a service delayed sometimes for two years; perhaps because of weather or a lack of funds, perhaps because the family seeks to find a minister of their own denomination who will come up the rugged creek and officiate at the ceremony. With the long postponement, odd situations are always arising. I know of one funeralizing where a husband was compelled to wait so long after the death of his wife, he had already taken a new bride and been married a year before his friends could gather with him to pray at the grave of the departed. The person who wept the loudest of all the mourners was the new wife.

Up another pine-shaded stream where a man had been killed in an argument, the family of the dead man after many months had at last found a satisfactory preacher; but they still needed someone to read out the lines of the hymns. It was a region remote from any school; the only individual near by who could read was the man who had done the killing. The family hesitated a long time before asking for his help, then with much reluctance, finally made the request. The services began, and were proceeding as usual, when some of the relatives of the deceased objected to the tone in which the killer was saying the words of the sacred songs. The funeralizing halted abruptly. And only the frantic efforts of the preacher prevented half a dozen new fatalities.

There are many devotees of the Holiness Church, better known to outsiders as the Holy Rollers. Some of the members are "snake handlers," who play with giant rattlers; others are "flame handlers," who lift red-hot stoves and burning lamps, all to show their faith.

These practices may seem odd to the uninitiated. Yet the worshipers are sincere, kindly folk, who somehow find here the expression of their spiritual needs. In a little church I attended, the preacher, after the congregation had been leaping about wildly for a quarter of an hour, began to talk in a quiet voice.

"People wants to know why us Holiness Folks git like this," he told his listeners. "Why we git so happy singing and dancing. I'll tell you how it is. It's thisaway.

"The other day I seen a fellow holding a string. 'What you holding that string for, brother?' I asked him.

'I'm a flying a kite,' he said.

'I can't see no kite,' I answered. 'Can you see the kite?'

'No, brother, I can't see it,' he told me. 'It's too high up in the air for me to see it. But I can sure feel it tugging.'

"That's the way it is with Holiness Church."

The administration of justice in the isolated areas still surprises the visitor with its differences from the ways of the towns. Despite a few modern touches, a cuspidor or two missing, or the presence of some young lawyers fresh from the state university, a mountain trial is in spirit much the same as when I first visited the Cumberlands thirty years ago, and court was opened with an old fiddler's contest. A court session is still the great event of the year.

It is the informality, like so many other phases of mountain life, which instantly charms the visitor.

I was in a mountain court one afternoon, sitting on the bench with the judge as he prepared to swear in the annual Grand Jury.

The jurist turned to the tobacco-munching farmers arranged solemnly before him on a double row of chairs. "Before I swear you in, I want to ask you," he said. "Is there anybody sitting here that's under indictment for anything? I don't want nobody on my jury that's under indictment."

There was a long silence. Then on the back row a lanky farmer arose, and shifted uneasily. "Guess they got me up in federal court over at Maysville for moonshining, Judge."

The judge shook his head in regret. "You got to get off the Grand Jury, then, Jeff. I ain't going to have nobody on my jury that's under indictment."

One of the most popular figures in the hills today is known as Judge Honey, a philosopher always more concerned with the right and wrong of a case than with the harsh technicality of the law. Whoever it may be that appears before him for sentence, whether solemn old man or impudent young woman, the judge always addresses the prisoner as "honey."

"Honey, I hate to do this to you," he declares. "But I've got to sentence you to sixty days, honey."

It seems to make the punishment easier to bear.

A mountain jail has the same homey quality. The jailer has been a neighbor and often a friend of most of his charges; the usual grimness of a prison is altogether lacking. In one mountain town the county jailer, a most amiable soul, took my wife and myself on a tour, carefully introducing us to each of his forty-seven prisoners. We shook hands with them all, including two held for murder.

So easygoing is the administration of justice, I have more than once heard a sheriff ask a mountaineer from some distant creek to inform a neighbor that he was under arrest and tell him to be sure to come to jail as soon as possible. And he could be certain the arrested man would obey, just as surely as if the sheriff went to his cabin and himself applied a pair of handcuffs. The mountaineer has great reverence for his own local authorities. He has none for laws made by people he has never seen in far-off Washington.

Mountain politics, like the courts, have suffered some outward changes. The politician may buy time on the local radio to denounce his opponents; he may have his picture printed on a lurid-colored fan. But basically he is the same colorful figure as the candidate I once met with the uncomplicated platform: "A dog for every man in the mountains."

One self-effacing citizen in a settlement I visited had a

Chicago Public Library
Rogers Park
5/20/2013   2:04:50 PM
-Patron Receipt-

ITEMS BORROWED:

1:
Title: Tried by war : Abraham Lincoln as c
Item #: R0415270892
Due Date: 6/10/2013

-Please retain for your records-

JHUI

singular plea for election. "Everybody knows," he told his hearers, "that we don't need no county attorney in this county. You vote for me and I'll make you as near none as you ever had."

Competition in a campaign reaches an intensity unknown in other areas, though pistols do not crack as often as in the old days. One marked change has taken place in the politician's mode of travel. The young mountaineers learned about the jeep in the Army, and bringing it back to their own stony hollows, used it where before they had used only horse or mule. The vehicle proved singularly adapted to the needs of the candidate for office. So many politicians in jeeps now come down the creeks seeking votes, the mountaineers say before an election that the hills have broken out with "jeep fever."

Medical practices have altered considerably, due to the work of the schools and the medical centers established occasionally on some far-off mountainside. But there are still vast areas without a doctor anywhere. The medical men in the booming coal towns are too overburdened with patients to ride about the country succoring the sick, as was the custom of their predecessors in a more placid time. The result is that many of the cures of an earlier generation are not forgotten. Babies are still treated for a throat infection called thrash by having a man who has never seen his father breathe into the sick infant's mouth. A treatment for fever is to split onions and place them under the patient's bed. The fever will pass into the onions, an event made visible by their turning black.

In one area the medical problems were solved in unusual fashion. The doctor was an old man very popular along the winding creeks he traveled. But as I talked to him, at times I was puzzled. His manner and methods seemed to differ sharply from the ways of the conventional practitioner. And then one day I discovered the reason. Years before he had been sentenced to a long term of prison for moonshining; he had learned his doctoring when he became a male nurse in "The Walls"—the federal penitentiary.

The mountaineer beyond the towns is still a member of a close-knit community. He helps the newly married son of a near-by farmer build a cabin. He lends a neighbor his plow or his horse, and farms that neighbor's land if sickness comes; he would be shocked if he were offered a penny. Often he is actually a relative; in many a county the majority of the inhabitants all bear the name of the same family. In one county the last names of seven hundred and seventy-five taxpayers are identical; since each taxpayer represents a group, the actual number of persons called by the same family termination is probably three thousand. This out of a total population of perhaps five thousand.

Since there are only a few common first names—Jack, Henry, Luke, John—affairs might well be in a state of complete confusion. But the mountaineer has solved the problem in his own easy rustic fashion. A man is not known as Bob Boling, or Hardin, or Sizemore, or Creech; there might be sixty Bob Bolings or Hardins in the county he calls home. Instead, when a boy he is given a nickname, which clings to him throughout his life. He is Catslap Bob or Butterlip Bob or Shoot-er-Right Bob or Shoot-er-Straight Bob; when the nickname is spoken, no one doubts for an instant which particular Bob is intended.

His immediate family the mountaineer loves with intense devotion. Often stoic, reserved, like so many untutored men who feel deeply, he may make little outward show of his affection. He may rarely kiss his wife or daughter; he may not even press his son's hand as the youth goes off on some long journey. But he would gladly toil from dawn to dawn if it would give them health or wealth or learning; he would without hesitation sacrifice his life if it were vital to their happiness.

And as he loves his family, so he loves his hills. To some farmers there is no beauty in the land they till; for them it is merely unwilling clay out of which by their labors they must wring a livelihood. The hillman is conscious of the beauty of his country every moment. He will describe to you like a poet the charm of the dark hills rising before his cabin—the pines atop Saddleback or the Breaks o' Sandy. He is lost when he is away.

I was taking a trip once on a crowded bus, traveling west from the city of Washington, when I chanced to talk with a fellow passenger, a middle-aged man from the heart of the Cumberlands. For years it had been his ambition to see the capital of his country; at last he had accumulated enough to stay for a week in the metropolis. Carefully he made his plans, and setting out on the voyage, arrived without incident at the Washington depot. But when he went into the street and saw no hills anywhere, only a mass of honking automobiles and rushing humanity, a wave of nostalgia swept him for the country that he loved and understood.

"I seen a bus waiting outside the door," he told me, as we rolled on through the Virginia hills. "And the driver standing there said it was heading back to the mountains. So I give him my ticket and went aboard her. I'm sure glad I'm going home."

Some mountain men, unlike this short-lived tourist, do become travelers. The regular army always numbers many mountain boys. Others go off to work in the factories of the cities, Louisville and St. Louis, Cincinnati and Detroit. Some of the younger ones remain and adapt themselves to the new environment. The older ones are unhappy every moment until they come back to their little mountain farms, where they can once more watch the white-flecked streams coursing down the stony valleys, and hear the wind murmuring its hushed symphony in the pines.

Yet it is a hard life to which they always seek to return. The mountaineer has no money, no luxuries. His wallpaper is often the pages of a magazine, pasted over the cracks between the great logs to keep out the wind and the sun and the cold; his food, when Nature is in a niggardly mood, is barely enough to sustain life until the next season. This gives him a pathetic interest in little things, those trifles which are a routine part of the lives of the people in the towns. A post card of New York which held up to a lamp shows the windows of the skyscrapers lighted at night, a spoon marked Souvenir of Miami, are treasures beyond price, to be shown to every visitor. The arrival of a cake or a cheap pair of shoes for the daughter's baby, sent by some relative gone off to a factory, is an event to be discussed for months.

A friend of mine, the head of a Cumberland school, went each year on a strange mission. A mountaineer from an unusually isolated area sold some timber in a town at the mouth of the river along which his land was lying; urged on by a shrewd salesman, he used the money he received to purchase a piano for his little daughter. After a voyage of many days on a barge, he brought the **piano** to the muddy river landing that lay near-

est his home. He and his neighbors, after herculean labor, at last succeeded in carrying it across the rough ridges to his cabin.

And then he discovered there was no one in the near-by hills who could play.

For thirty years the piano stood there, mute, unopened

until my friend of the mountain school happened to ride past and stopped for water. Hesitantly the mountaineer, now gray haired with the passing of time, asked if she could play the instrument. When she answered in the affirmative, at the whole family's urging she sat down on the polished stool. For several hours she played, until her hands were weary. She returned each year thereafter to give a similar concert. And the faces of her auditors lighted as though they had seen Paradise.

As with most simple folk, music plays an important part in the lives of the mountain dwellers. The lucky traveler may still on rare occasions come upon a "singing," a gathering of the neighbors from the surrounding hollows, who will all day chant their favorite melodies as they chanted in the olden times, long before the advent of the phonograph and the radio.

Often when I have wandered through the area, I have taken a mandolin; it was a key that unlocked every cabin door.

It has led me into some pleasant adventures with local musicians, whose king is the old-time mountain fiddler. Though the old fiddler tunes his violin differently for almost every piece he plays, he manages to make all the pieces sound exactly alike.

I met Fiddling Jack, the bearded musical master of his valley.

We talked a moment in the little crossroads store where we were gathered; then Fiddling Jack took up his violin.

"Play *Fire on the Mountain,* Jack," called a gaunt farmer, sitting near the doorway, and Jack fiddled valiantly.

"Play *Billy Boy,*" spoke up the gaunt man, and a second solo followed. I listened, and at first could not believe my ears. As far as I could distinguish, the fiddle was again playing *Fire on the Mountain.*

A third and fourth solo came in quick succession. I could not detect the difference of a single note.

It was time for the fifth number. Fiddling Jack looked at my mandolin thoughtfully. "Let's you and me play a duet, brother," he said.

The only piece we both knew was *Old Kentucky Home.* I tuned my mandolin, and began to strum the melody. I had been trilling away with enthusiasm for a moment, when I noticed that something was terribly wrong with our intended harmony. I stopped my playing and listened. The fiddle was scraping out *Fire on the Mountain.*

I play duets no more.

Often I have puzzled over the reason for the extraordinary similarity of these mountain tunes. I think the cause probably lies in the musicians' illiteracy. Unable to read or write, with no transcribed music, and no other recorded instructions, the mountain minstrel handed down the songs only by ear from one generation to another; in the process all the tunes blurred and merged, until any single melody became unrecognizable.

Once this mountain music proved a boon to the player. I chanced to visit an upland jail where a genial individual known as Stringy Bob was a valued resident, serving a considerable term because of some carelessness in his moonshining. An accomplished musician in the native fashion, he had fashioned a guitar out of a cigar box to while away the time; all afternoon he entertained me and his prison mates with a rich store of doleful songs. Several days later court was opened, accompanied as usual by an old fiddlers' contest. My praise of Stringy Bob was so enthusiastic, he was permitted to leave jail and enter the competition. From the moment of his appearance there was no doubt of the result; the judges without consultation awarded him first prize. Next day, though his sentence still had several months to run, I saw him walking about the town, wearing the tight, white duck suit borrowed for his recital. The music-loving authorities had properly decided that the community's leading talent could not be thwarted by prison bars, and had given Stringy Bob his liberty.

The language of the mountaineers itself has a musical quality. It is logical that the old ballads should here be best preserved. The names of the creeks, the settlements, have extraordinary color and picturesqueness: Hell For Certain, a rocky creek that is still a bitter trial for man or horse or mule; Troublesome Creek, which needs no defining; Hoopfalari, where a ghost comes flying out from a cave in a mountain, uttering the weird cry "Whoop For Larry"; Burnt Camp Creek and Little Double; Travelers Rest and Gobblers Knob. The speech is full of rustic poetry. Not long ago I heard a judge remark of a girl whose husband he had just sentenced: "She drove her ducks to a bad market."

Here and there an older word crops out that has not been in use for many years, sometimes giving rise to the impression that the natives of the Cumberlands speak Elizabethan English. It is still not unusual in a grocery store equipped with the newest scales from Toledo and the latest cash register from Dayton to hear a clerk ask a customer buying apples: "Do you want 'em in a poke?"

The hillman's amusements are unsophisticated as his music. In remote districts the visitor can still find a turkey shoot or beef match, the latter a shooting competition for a steer. But perhaps the oddest survival is the fox race. This is not a fox hunt. On the contrary, if the fox happens to be captured, the offending dog and dog owner go off in disgrace.

A group of perhaps ten or twenty of the more sportive mountain men, accompanied by hounds of all varieties, go out at night to the top of a hill where a fox is known to be prowling. Soon the dogs are loosed and take up the noisy chase. Their masters sit and listen intently to their barking, each man knowing the cry of his dog as a devoted father knows the voice of his child. Just as the owner of a prize-winning horse follows with his eyes its course around a race track, the tense dog owners follow with their ears the coursing of their hounds through the darkness.

"That's Amos a-coming first around the hill yonder!" shouts one enthusiastic master.

"You mean he was first," calls another. "'Cause Grobey's passing him right now."

"Going to be Fats beats 'em all," says a figure in the shadows. "Ain't no dog alive can beat Fats."

Devotees of the sport have been known to stay away from home three days and nights at a time in this fashion.

"Ain't worth two cents to nobody, all this fox racing," an old mountaineer told me dryly. "Excepting to the fox. 'Cause ain't nothing tickles a fox like seeing a human acting a fool."

The mountaineer's character is perhaps best illustrated by the episode of Uncle William, whom I met years ago when I first tramped the Cumberlands. It at once demonstrates the hillman's striking individuality and his consuming interest in the little things of life; above all it shows his tenacity, his "divine stubbornness" in being unwilling ever to admit defeat.

Back in the days when I knew him, Uncle William was the sage of Pine Mountain; he was the leader to whom the creek dwellers far and near turned for guidance in time of decision. In any rural community the mail is always a matter of importance, particularly a region so isolated as the Cumberlands. Uncle William had decided that Pine Mountain's crying need was a post office.

For years he had labored so that letters could come to the little cabins that dotted the green hollows. At every attempt his efforts foundered on the stern government rule that no office could be opened until the postal business in the area reached a certain definite total each year.

Uncle William at last grew weary of delay and failure. He decided to take drastic action; when Uncle William took action a result was as certain as night follows day.

The difficulty in the great postal war was that most of Uncle William's neighbors could neither read nor write; mail is after all a form of written communication. He made a first attack on the problem by calling at every mountain cabin; solemnly he urged each mountaineer to send off to both of the leading mail-order houses for their catalogues. If the son-in-law of the family had a different name, he asked the farmer to send off twice. Whenever the necessity arose, which was often, he wrote the cards of request himself.

This initial undertaking produced a considerable postal volume; each heavy catalogue that arrived was balm to Uncle William's soul. His next move in the campaign was in the more complicated field of correspondence. The First World War had come upon the countryside; most of the young men were away in the Army. Uncle William made the rounds of the cabins again, urging mothers to write to their sons and daughters to their sweethearts. Here again the lack of formal learning interfered with their desires. Once more Uncle William became the correspondent, writing long letters telling the news of the day. When the answers came, scrawled by some soldier friend of the absent one, he would journey to the cabin and read it aloud to the whole family.

So effective were his efforts that even the postal authorities in charge of the district were impressed by the quantity of mail that was arriving. At last they decided the business was enough to warrant opening the office.

Uncle William restrained his joy.

But then a new problem arose as he talked over the matter with the officials who came from a distant city to investigate. The young men were all off at the war. There was no one left to make the arduous journey from the end of the railroad down in the valley and bring the mail across the mountain; no one to carry it up the twisting creeks and branches where at times the water almost hid the rider's saddle.

Uncle William thought a long time over the question. He was now an old man who had earned his hours of leisure; his limbs were no longer fitted for fighting the stern mountains.

Then he spoke to the postal officials with resolution. "I'll carry the mail myself," he said.

For years after he could be seen going through the hills with his heavy mailbags, sometimes on horseback, sometimes on foot, his wrinkled face glowing with the satisfaction of a mission accomplished; he had brought the post office to Pine Mountain.

There are many Uncle Williams still in the Cumberlands; it is their presence which makes these hazy uplands unique. For they are the last outposts of a vanished world.

The mountaineer has many faults. He is quick to take offense, he is sometimes violent. But his virtues far outweigh his sins. He is kind, he is honest, he is loyal to the death. He takes no man's orders and gives orders to no man. His single aim in life is to be free.

In twenty or thirty years, perhaps, he will have disappeared, his only trace a headstone on some pine-bordered hill. Yet as long as America lasts he will live on in spirit. For he is Daniel Boone and Simon Kenton and the men with the coonskin caps that wandered the trackless forests and tamed the wilderness. He is the flatboatmen and the raftsmen and the pilots and the mates who steered their craft past rapids and shoals to build a new country at the mouth of the Mississippi. He is the mule-men and the oxmen and the weather-beaten guides who took the covered wagons across the plains of the West.

He is the pioneer who made America.

BALLAD OF PINY RIDGE

Oh, a-ridin', a-ridin' down a piny lane,
    The moon is over my head, Lord;
I spied a-walkin', a-walkin' Davie Mayne—
    How long, O Lord, how long?

Oh, he's walkin', he's talkin' with my true love fair,
    The clouds are over my head, Lord;
His hands are kissin', a-kissin' her gold hair—
    How long, O Lord, how long?

Oh, I whipped, oh, I whipped my pistol from my side,
    The darkness over my head, Lord;
I shot young Davie, young Davie till he died—
    How long, O Lord, how long?

Oh, the sheriffs, the sheriffs bound me down with steel,
    The noose is over my head, Lord;
My mother, my mother's a-weepin' as I kneel—
    How long, O Lord, how long?

THE COBBS AN' McFARLANDS ARE FIGHTIN'

The McFarlands are fightin', they're fightin' the Cobbs;
They've come down from Big Smoky, come down from the
    Knobs.
        Oh, the Cobbs an' McFarlands are fightin'!

Oh, there's fourteen McFarlands, of Cobbs there's eighteen;
They've met by the willows, they've dropped to the green.
        Oh, the Cobbs an' McFarlands are fightin'!

Oh, the black-browed McFarlands shoot bullets of steel,
An' in their hearts' blood seven Cobbs silent kneel.
        Oh, the Cobbs an' McFarlands are fightin'!

Oh, the flaxen-haired Cobb men shoot bullets of lead,
An' on the red grass six McFarlands lie dead.
        Oh, the Cobbs an' McFarlands are fightin'!

Children of Noah

Down the trail spur gray horsemen with saddles dust white;
On their gallopin' shoulders long rifles hang bright.
      Oh, the Cobbs an' McFarlands are fightin'!

The McFarlands cease firin'; the Cobbs to them shout:
" 'Tis the rev'nuers comin'! The marshals are out!"
      When the Cobbs an' McFarlands were fightin'.

Oh, the Cobbs an' McFarlands they lie side by side,
With rifles fierce flamin' the rev'nuers ride,
      When the Cobbs an' McFarlands were fightin'.

A McFarland has fallen, his face dyes the ground;
A Cobb man has caught him, an' quick the hurt bound,
      When the Cobbs an' McFarlands were fightin'.

Oh, a Cobb man sinks down to the hot smokin' clay,
A McFarland's black fingers the wellin' blood stay,
      When the Cobbs an' McFarlands were fightin'.

Oh, the marshals turn back to the darkenin' plain;
But many's the rider in saddle rides slain,
      When the Cobbs an' McFarlands were fightin'.

Oh, there's four left of Cobb men, McFarlands there's three;
They've forgot the gray marshals, they've dropped to the knee.
      Oh, the Cobbs an' McFarlands are fightin'!

The McFarlands shoot steel an' the Cobb men shoot lead,
An' on the green moss the McFarlands are dead.
    Oh, the Cobb men have beat the McFarlands!

OH, THEY'RE SEEKIN' JAMIE TOLLIVER

Oh, they're weepin' up in Hyden town, in Hyden on the hill,
Oh, they're shoutin' up in Hyden, but a woman's voice is still;
Oh, there's farmers' men an' sheriff's men an' silent soldiers
three,
Oh, they're seekin' Jamie Tolliver to deck the gallows-tree.

Young Jamie's in the mistin' woods, he's on the veilin' peak,
He's stealin' through the piny glen, he's glidin' down the
creek;
He's creepin' o'er the tricklin' stones, he's won the river's
shore,
He's spied a leakin' wooden boat an' spied a broken oar.

The farmers' men they guard the woods an' see him mount
the peak,
The sheriff's men they guard the glen an' hear him win the
creek,
But the soldiers three stand silently an' watch the river's shore;
They've caught young Jamie Tolliver an' barred the prison
door.

The lawyers' men, the lawyers' men are robed in robes of
  gray,
But the judges' men, the judges' men all robed in black are
  they:
"Now hark to us and heed to us and plead to us your plea,
Else you shall hang like withered leaf upon the gallows-tree."

Young Jamie's laughed a bitter laugh an' proud he's raised his
  head:
"This world will be a sweeter place when judges' men are
  dead.
The Lord has carven down in stone. 'Take for an eye an eye.'
Men's laws are false as crawlin' snake, but God's laws do not
  lie.

"Oh, high an' far's my cabin gray an' wild an' fair's my land.
An' free my life till the sheriff came an' smilin' shook my
  hand.
He's written in a book of red an' taxed my plowin' ground;
He's written in a book of black an' taxed my huntin' hound.

"Oh, dear to the mountain man's the peak a-smoke in the sun-
  set fog,
An' dear the birds in the hummin' pines, but dearer than all's
  his dog.
No tax they lay on leapin' deer nor tax on laughin' child;
An' evil 'tis to tax the hound was born when Jesus smiled.

Children of Noah

"The city men they bow the head an' tremblin' bend the knee,
But the mountains know no law but God's, the mountain man
   is free.
I paid in silver cool as milk the toll upon my ground;
But I paid in words as hot as blood the taxes on my hound.

"The sheriff's breathed a bitter breath an' filled his gun with
   lead,
But I looked down the shinin' road where waits his son, young
   Jed.
'There stands your youngest lad so dear. On him no toll you
   pay;
Before I pay a tax on hound white in my grave I'll lay!'

"The sheriff's leaped his stampin' horse, he's galloped down
   the glen,
But he rode once more with riders four an' four of county
   men.
Oh, woe's to me an' woe's to him the trait'rous deed did do;
When I was down in Hyden town my faithful hound he slew.

"Oh, long I looked an' gray I looked till night the gray sky
   won,
I rode like wolf to Hyden town, I shot the sheriff's son.
An' hear you, judges' men so black, to you I plead my plea:
The mountains know no law but God's—I followed his
   decree."

Oh, they're weepin' up in Hyden town, in Hyden on the hill,

Oh, they're shoutin' up in Hyden, but there's many a voice is still.

Oh, there's sheriff's men an judges' men an' silent soldiers three;

Oh, they're hangin' smilin' Jamie—for the mountain man is free.

CHILDREN OF NOAH: A RUSTIC COMEDY

River was so deep and wide
I couldn't call my baby from the other side
— RIVER SONG

CHILDREN OF NOAH

Eb witcher stopped working in his yard, and glanced at the six gaping children clinging to the picket fence before his weather-beaten cottage. Tall and silvery haired, his lanky body was covered with a pair of worn overalls; the upper part of the garment was spotted startlingly here and there with red as his undershirt showed through an occasional hole.

Wiping his great white mustaches with the fragment of shirt which served him as handkerchief, he reflected on what a weighty fraction of Caney Corners' population these peering children of the Widow Marvin represented. The hamlet's residents totaled only fourteen even when counting the twins as two, a mathematical calculation over which he had puzzled, and which the widow herself had pointed out as an inaccuracy to the stubborn census taker who had come from up the river several months before. He looked at the sign above the door which proclaimed him a junk dealer, then turned away to study the paintless store adjoining of Ruby Corkell, the druggist. A moment later he let his gaze rest on the dilapidated dwelling belonging to Sandy Tackett, the broommaker, visible some distance away. He pondered how the settlement's strategic position on a crossroads near the Mississippi made it possible that three of its five buildings could be thus devoted to commerce and industry.

At length his meditations ended. Picking up a saw, he was cutting a thick timber when a voice hailed him from beyond the yard. An old man carying a bundle of brooms on his back had joined the group of children, a figure wearing a faded blue jacket adorned with five enormous mother-of-pearl buttons and a beribboned straw hat which looked as if at one time it had belonged to a girl. The newcomer's hair was silvery as the junk dealer's, seeming even whiter because of his long beard.

"Have a good trip, Sandy?" the junkman called out without ceasing from his labor.

The aged visitor, who was Mr. Tackett, the neighboring broommaker, did not answer. He was staring at an enormous wooden structure beside which Eb was toiling and which appeared to occupy most of his modest yard; an uncouth framework of ribs and stays rising to a height of perhaps ten feet and stretching out to a length of thirty. It resembled the skeleton of some prehistoric monster being mounted in a museum. All about it were piles of rough-sawed timbers, some kegs of nails, a half dozen rolls of tar-paper, and a few coils of rusty wire.

Continuing to preserve his silence, Sandy took out a pair of chipped eyeglasses, and setting them against his forehead, peered out incredulously. "Sakes a-mighty, Eb," he called at length. "What you making there?"

The junkman scraped some sweat from his arm with the back of the saw. "What does it look like I'm making?" he retorted.

The newcomer removed his girlish hat and scratched his snowy head. "Maybe you're making a shantyboat?"

Eb looked at him in disgust and chalked a line on a wide plank. "It's a ark," he grunted.

Sandy's beard seemed to flutter. He opened the rickety gate before the junkman's cottage, and plodded up the brick walk until he was at the other's side. "I ain't exactly understood you, Eb. My hearing ain't as good as it used to be. What is it you say you're building?"

"I said I was building a ark."

"I hear you. But I sure can't understand you, Eb."

"*Ark*. A-r-k. Like Noah's ark. That's plain English, ain't it? You understand now?"

Sandy folded up his glasses and solemnly restored them to their case. "Why you making it?"

"I got to make it. I seen a vision." He began sawing the plank along the chalked line. "Seen it last month. Just a couple of days after you went away. It was a Tuesday." Some sawdust dropped unheeded into his muddy boots. "I was fishing on the river. Down at Four Mile near that big maple where the blacksnakes always comes. You know the place. I was out in Lem Kroger's boat. Fished all day and didn't come home till dark, I was catching so many. Caught three big buckets. I fried some of 'em, ate hearty, and went to bed. And I hadn't no more than got to sleep when I seen him."

"Seen who?"

"The angel. I was out on the river again, like in the afternoon. It was just the same, Lem's boat, the big maple on the shore, and the fish buckets, and everything. I was sitting in the stern, and he come in the bow. He looked round for a minute like he was kind of getting his bearings, and then he sat down, same as me or you. He was wearing a dress made of white silk, all shiny, with gold braid around the edges, prettier than any braid they got in the store down at Granny Run. In one hand he was holding a trumpet like that fellow plays in the moving picture show, and in the other he was holding a big book. That was all gold, too. 'Don't you waste your time fishing no more, Eb Witcher,' he says to me. 'All the time you got to spare you're going to use in building a ark, just like Noah did. Caney Corners gets floods every year, but this year a flood's coming that'll make all the others look like nothing. If you knew anything about the way the bark's growing on the trees you could see that without my telling you. You're just a junk dealer and you ain't a godly man and I don't know why you was chosen but you was. You got to save the people of Caney Corners when the flood comes.' Then he opens the book and right there in the middle of it he shows me my name. It was written in gold, too. Mighty pretty, I tell you, seeing EBENEZER WITCHER written out all in gold letters. Then he closed the book and flew away, and I woke up. Now you see why I'm building it?"

Sandy dipped his hand into a paper bag he was holding and withdrew a small peppermint cane of the sort hung on Christmas trees. He bit off a piece and began to munch it soberly. "Said anything to Parson Robbins about this?"

"What I got to do with Parson Robbins? I ain't been to meeting at Granny Run for five years."

"Noah's the Bible, and anything's the Bible is the parson's."

Eb accepted a fragment of candy. "Widow Marvin's sister said something about it to him, and he ain't said nothing one way or the other." His drawling voice became touched with sulkiness. "But Deacon Clifty hold her to warn me about what I was doing. Said if I wanted to call it a shantyboat, it was alright. But if I called it a ark, I was a infidel."

Sandy's eyes roamed up and down the whalelike hulk. "I seen lots smarter people than Deacon Clifty."

Eb plucked a crumb of candy from his imposing mustache. "You're sure right. When a angel tells me to do something,

I'm going to do it, no matter what no two-by-four little deacon says. It'll be a fine-looking ark, too, before I'm through."

"It'll be a shanty, Eb. It can't be no ark." The broom-maker's words were mild, but emphatic.

"It's a ark, I tell you."

"You're stubborner than a Georgia mule, Eb. Can't you see it can't be no ark? Your name ain't Noah, is it? You ain't got no sons named Shem and Ham, have you? No matter how many angels you seen it wouldn't be no ark. Not even if they built it with their own hands for you. There's only one ark. That was Noah's. There can't be no more anywhere. Deacon Clifty was right. Even if he ain't smart most of the time." He shifted the brooms on his back, preparatory to taking his departure. "Besides, I'm as good at telling weather as anybody, and I don't figure the flood this year's going to be bigger than the others anyways."

"You wait and see. You'll be just as glad as the rest of 'em to get on when the time comes."

"I won't, Eb. And even if I did, it'd be a shanty just the same. A good shanty. But just a shanty."

Eb wiped the saw on his overalls. His bronzed face tightened. The ends of his mustache uplifted. "Me and you's been friends for a long time and I thought you had more sense than some of these other folks living in Caney Corners, Mr. Tackett," he announced coldly. "But I see you ain't. And a important man like you must be too busy to go ahead wasting time talking to a man as big a fool as me."

Sandy made no response and started toward the gate.

Eb picked up a hammer. "I'm sorry I ate your candy," he went on gloomily. "If I could, I'd give it back. I don't want to take no favors from you." He placed the plank which he had been cutting against a beam and began to nail it fast. "It was good candy. Peppermint candy you get nowadays down at Granny Run ain't what it used to be. Melts up to nothing in a second. This kind lasts. Where'd you get it?"

Sandy's wrinkled visage brightened. He drew the half-eaten cane out of its sack once more. "Store down near my brother's place at Goose Island where I was staying. All the candy's good there. Have another chunk?"

"Not unless you say it's a ark."

The old man shook his head regretfully, and trudged up the road.

The place he had occupied at the fence was taken a few minutes later by another visitor, a stocky, amiable figure with a broad face out of which shone several flashing gold teeth. He wore no hat, his head being covered with a mass of unruly red hair. About his clothes clung a peculiar medicinal odor which branded him instantly as Ruby Corkell, the owner of the drugstore next door.

He leaned over the fence pickets to get a clear view of the operations in the yard. "How's the shanty coming today?" he called jovially.

The junkman did not look up from the board he was planing.

"You're getting mighty impolite these days, Eb," the druggist asserted. "What's the matter with you? Ain't you talking to people no more?"

"When people calls things by their right names I'll talk to 'em." Stonily the junkman pulled out a wooden shaving which was clogging the plane. "If your eyes is so bad you can't tell the difference between a ark and a shantyboat, I'm sorry for you. You better take some of your stale medicine and treat 'em with it."

"You ain't talking to nobody what won't call it a ark?"

"I sure ain't."

A grasshopper lit upon the druggist's arm. He brushed it away. "You ain't going to do much talking then. You can't make yourself nobody out of the Bible. All the people here says it, and all the people down at Granny Run says it. Some of 'em says a curse'll come on you for it. But that ain't the way I figure. The Lord ain't going to bother his head none just 'cause a junkman's making a fool of himself. . . . Judge Lacey come in the store last night. You know what the judge is saying?"

"Still talking about the time he shook hands with the President in Washington, I guess. Never talks about nothing else."

"Alright, but he's saying more. That's what I come over to tell you. He says you're disgracing Caney Corners. Says if you keep it up you ought to be put in a lunatic asylum. Says if you keep it up he'll see about getting out papers."

He lingered a moment to see if this conclusive announcement would provoke a rejoinder, but finding that it failed, turned and walked back to his shop.

Eb chalked a new line on another piece of lumber. He was nailing it into position where it apparently was to form part of a window frame, when a bright-painted buggy neared the great beech tree that grew before the cottage. In the jaunty vehicle sat Judge Lacey. The judge had never presided in a courtroom. He was, however, a deputy in the office of the county clerk at Granny Run; his neighbors felt that this office amply justified the higher and more dignified title, even without considering his other varied political activities. He was visibly the richest and most important of Caney Corners' inhabitants. He was fat in the fashion that only politicians can be fat, with a stomach swollen like a watermelon. His suit was unpatched and cut in an attempt to be fashionable. His shirt was carefully pressed. His black hat was wide brimmed like that of the near-by plantation owners. His shoes were shined.

Judge waved a whip as the buggy drove past, then grinned broadly when the carpenter turned away his head.

"Says I'm a lunatic, does he?" Eb muttered to himself as he watched the vehicle disappear round a corner of the Widow Marvin's trim cottage. "Says I'm disgracing Caney Corners. Alright. We'll see what he'll be saying when the flood comes."

He put away his tools to go inside the house and prepare

〰〰〰205

some turnip greens and corn bread. The meal over, he strode into the yard again to resume his labors.

For a long time afterward he could be found there every day, sawing and hammering, until darkness forced him into a starry retreat. Of necessity his business as a junkman was neglected. But hour by hour the wooden monster grew. The stout wooden ribs were covered and became a hull. A cabin divided into two unequal sections took form and sloped up to a sharply peaked roof. A thin pole too light to be a mast appeared in the square-nosed bow. As Eb worked, his relations with the censorious male members of the community ceased entirely. The women, however, unwilling to lose a market for some castoff bit of furniture or a possible opportunity of picking up some useful utensil from his stores, concealed their disapproval.

At last the huge vessel was completed and covered with a coat of flaming crimson. Over the door of the smaller compartment of the cabin Eb painted the single word FOLKS, over the larger the word CRITTURS.

Using the same brush, he decorated the hull with the names of what he considered celebrated biblical characters. Completely around the boat they ran as a sort of frieze on the scarlet gunwale: Joshua, Jeremiah, Deuteronomy, Solomon, Daniel, Exodus, Job. Parson Robbins, hastily summoned by the neighbors from Granny Run, convinced him for the moment that this was truly sacrilege. The offending names were erased.

For a month the craft lay in the tall green grass of the yard, like a scarlet whale floating on an emerald sea, to the scorn or delight of all who passed on the highway. Then late one afternoon a heavy rain began to fall. The deluge, once begun, continued without slackening, as though a sluice gate had been opened which could not be closed. Rumors began to be heard of a flood farther up the river. In this there was nothing extraordinary. Caney Corners was one of those many settlements in the Mississippi Valley where floods were looked upon as a necessary and yearly evil. Each spring the inhabitants packed up their possessions and trundled them in wagons over the road to the higher land at Granny Run. There they would wait until the water had subsided, then come back to their still-damp houses and begin sweeping out the mud.

Two weeks passed and the rain gave no sign of lessening. The flood rumors increased. Eb moved some of his furniture into the boat. His watching neighbors began to think of their annual migration. Then one morning they awakened to find that the rain had stopped, though the sky was filled with threatening clouds. Looking out their windows they saw that the slight rise on which the hamlet stood was an island in a vast-rolling sea of yellow water, an island which each moment grew smaller and smaller. This was astonishing. When the water had previously paid its muddy visits to Caney Corners it had risen gradually, allowing ample time for preparation and departure. Such rapidity was unheard of, almost incredible.

The Widow Marvin, who because of her numerous prog-
eny was generally the first in the hamlet to arise, hurried into
her yard. With her stiff-pigtailed eldest daughter she peered
off in the direction where the highway had stretched out over
the lowlands to Granny Run. All she could see was a surging
waste of brown.

"Land alive," she exclaimed to her daughter. "The levee
up at Poca must have busted. That's sure."

She was joined in a moment by the kimonoed sister who
shared her home, and five wide-eyed, half-buttoned children.
She saw in turn Sandy Tackett, Ruby Corkell, and Judge

Lacey come hastily out from their houses and stare as she had stared. She exchanged a few excited comments, then hurried through her gate to the dwelling of the junkman. She saw him before his whalelike craft, repainting the forbidden biblical names on the gunwale. His face was cleaner shaven than it had been in the memory of Caney Corners. Around his neck was a torturingly stiff collar fixed to an immaculate white shirt. On his head was a battered but still recognizable high silk hat, unmistakably drawn from his stock.

The widow repressed her surprise. "Water's sure come up sudden, ain't it, Eb?" she said nervously. "Wouldn't believe it if you couldn't see it with your own eyes. I come over to ask you if me and sister and the children can bring some of our things and come on board."

Eb bent down a corner of the collar which was digging deep into his unaccustomed flesh. He looked at her thoughtfully. "You can come on," he declared at length.

"Thank you, Eb. Got room for all of us, ain't you?"

"She'll hold plenty more than you."

A few moments later the widow and her now-buttoned brood began trooping onto the deck, laden down with gilt-framed pictures, starched bed linens, and neat mounds of children's garments. Eb showed the mother a corner of the interior where the burdens could be deposited, then with pride opened the door where above was inscribed the word CRITTURS. Here a row of stalls was exposed. In them stood Eb's horse, his cow, some bewildered ducks, a pair of dogs, and a sedate cat, the latter separated in such a manner as to make combat impossible.

"Angel didn't say nothing about taking on the animals," Eb explained. "But I figured he must have forgot, so I took 'em anyway. Angels can forget same as a human." He withdrew his handkerchief, and with it knocked off some sawdust which had fallen from the roof onto his shiny hat. "Ain't brought on my chickens yet. You can help me catch 'em if you want to."

He led the way down the boards which served as a gangplank, and stiff limbed because of a desire not to soil his clothes, was darting about the yard in pursuit of a few terrified fowl, when Judge Lacey's buggy, heaped high with bundles, drew up outside. Mud was already thick on the wheels, for the land where the judge's house lay a hundred yards down the road was somewhat lower than the general level of the village.

The politician climbed down awkwardly and came through the gate. "Lord a-mighty, how that water's rising," he panted. "Never seen anything like it in my born days. You got a place for me, ain't you, Eb?"

"Sure I got a place for you." The junkman's lean hand shot out and caught a chicken by the leg.

"Thank you a-mighty, Eb." Judge waddled toward the gangplank, curious to see the mysteries behind the open door.

With the chicken still in his hand, Eb hurried to the entrance and blocked the other's path. "Just a minute," he declared.

Judge's fat face fell. "What's the matter, Eb? You said I could come on board, didn't you?"

" 'Course I said you could come on board. But I want to find out a couple of things first."

"What you want to find out?"

"I want to know if you apologize for saying you was going to see about getting out lunatic papers for me."

Judge laughed feebly. "You ain't going to take a thing like that serious, are you, Eb? Why a baby that heard me when I said it would a-known I was joking."

"You apologize?" The slant of Eb's mustache was dogged.

" 'Course I apologize."

"Another thing I want to ask you. More important than apologizing even. Is it a shantyboat you're coming on? . . . Or is it a ark?"

Judge's beefy countenance lined with earnestness. " 'Course it's a ark, Eb. Ain't I been saying all the time it's a ark? You ask any of them people down at Granny Run. You don't know it maybe, but it was me took up for you when Deacon Clifty started talking against you."

The Widow Marvin, who stood listening near by, gasped at the audacity of the falsehood. Judge went on unruffled: "Can I get aboard now?"

"Yep."

"Got room for my horse and buggy, too, maybe? That buggy cost me a plenty of money."

"The horse can come. Buggy's got to stay. Buggy ain't got no place on a ark."

He resumed his pursuit of the chickens, then when all were safely deposited in the same stall as the ducks, walked to the fence and gazed at the water now licking at the wooden step in front of the dugstore.

Ruby Corkell, the proprietor, stood in the street piling up mountains of cardboard boxes and enveloping them in tablecloths and strips of burlap. He saw the junkman watching and hurried over. "Guess you got a place where you can put these boxes and me and the missus, maybe, ain't you, Eb?"

The junkman strode out to the edge of the rippling water and touched it experimentally with his shoe. "I guess maybe. . . . If it's a ark."

Ruby shifted uneasily. His usually amiable face hardened under his stormy red hair. "There ain't no room for me aboard your shanty then," he muttered.

His wife, a plump little woman wearing a flowered house dress, hurried forward. "What you riling him for, Ruby?" she demanded. "You know it's a ark. Anybody can see just by looking it's a ark." Then she whispered: "You're just plain crazy, Ruby. How you think you're going to get away from here if you don't go with him?"

"A shanty's a shanty," he replied stubbornly. "I ain't going to make a fool of myself for no man. Particular a man lives next door to me."

Mrs. Corkell glanced anxiously at the boxes piled before the store. "What you going to do about all those things then? Them new French perfumes and them talcum powders cost you so much money? I didn't know you was so rich you had dollar bills to throw in the water."

"Ain't dollar bills that counts. It's what's right. Besides when they find out what's happening here maybe they'll send out a boat from Granny Run."

"Tomorrow maybe, or the next day. They got more to do in a flood like this than think of Caney Corners. You're sure an awful fool sometimes, Ruby." Her chubby fingers tugged unhappily at the girdle of her dress. Then her glance darted to the shopwindow, past the gilded box of chocolates to be awarded for guessing the number of beans in a jar, to the odd clock overhead of the sort seen at county fairs, its body and dial a frying pan and its hands a knife and fork. Her face lit with inspiration. "What about that?" she flashed. "You going to let that get spoiled, too? You know if water just comes near the hands, it'll be finished quicker than lightning. There ain't another clock like that in a hundred miles of here. Maybe not in the whole state."

Ruby picked up a tube of tooth paste which had fallen onto the ground. He gazed at his wife mournfully and hesitated a moment, then gave a sigh and plodded into the store. Painstakingly he disengaged the bizarre timepiece from the hook on which it hung, then bearing it gently in his hands as though a jarring step or a sudden breath might destroy it, trudged into the road again.

Once more he sighed, bitterly. "All right," he said. "I guess it's a ark."

With his wife he began transporting their property to the ruddy leviathan, now groaning and muttering as if in protest against the many feet treading its deck.

Mrs. Corkell carried a shaded parlor lamp into the cabin and set it upon a layer of comforters. She looked admiringly at the heavy timbered roof and walls. "Nice place you got here, Eb," she declared. "Guess all of Caney Corners is on now, ain't they, excepting Sandy and Mrs. Tackett? Funny I ain't seen them all morning except for a minute when I first got up."

"I ain't neither," put in the Widow Marvin, near her. "Wonder what's keeping them. Maybe you getter go look, Eb."

"People wants to come on my ark knows where they can find it."

"I'll go, Ma," piped up the widow's pig-tailed eldest daughter.

"Think you better, honey. Maybe something's happened to 'em."

The child darted off and returned in a moment. "He says they ain't coming," she announced.

Eb grunted, and going into the other compartment, set

214

some straw before the horses. He emerged as the bearded Sandy appeared in the road, being propelled vigorously forward by a tall, long-boned woman smoking a clay pipe. With her free hand Mrs. Tackett was dragging a moth-eaten, apathetic mule. The trio slowed up at the gate of the cottage, and filing through, halted at the gangplank of the leviathan.

Mrs. Tackett gave her husband a final thrust. "Get on there now," she commanded, paying no attention to Eb, who stood watching dourly. "Mighty quick, too."

The little old broommaker shot forward. He halted just before he would have struck the junkman's stony form.

The proprietor of the craft continued to stand like a statue. "Just a minute, Mister Tackett." In his parleys with Judge and Ruby, Eb's voice had been touched with ponderous sarcasm; now it quivered in a very ecstasy of irony. "Just a minute, Professor." He thrust back the silk hat slipping dangerously from his head. "You and your mule and your wife is perfectly welcome to walk inside here. That's what I built it for. But before you come on I want to ask you something. I want to ask you particular because you're a man what knows all about everything; about the Bible, and encyclopedias, and dictionaries, and all the books and subjects there is. Leastways you did a couple of months ago. Now what I wants to ask you is a question about languages. I guess you knows a lot about languages. You must have studied Latin and Greek and maybe even Heberew when you was getting ready to be a broommaker."

He waved a hand toward his crimson giant. "I'll appreciate your telling me, Professor. I'm just a poor ignorant man myself and I ain't been lucky enough to go to all them colleges like you. So would you mind looking at this here and telling me. Is it a ark you're looking at or is it just a shanty? I know that ain't no easy question, Professor. But I ain't in no hurry. You can take all the time you need a-answering."

"I don't need no time," Sandy retorted as he turned to shuffle down the plank. "I know. It's a shanty."

His descent was checked by his grim-smoking wife. "I thought I told you to say it was a ark," she declared coldly.

"I ain't going to be a infidel or a liar for nobody."

"Going to sit in your house and drown?"

Sandy shrugged his shoulders. "I'll get away alright. Water ain't going to get much higher anyways. Besides I got my old boat I dragged up from the river last summer."

His wife angrily took the pipe from her browned teeth. "That boat ain't better than a cigar box. It'll sink the minute you touch it. You can go in it if you want to, but I won't. I'm going in Eb's ark."

She let the old man come down the plank past her, and thrusting the mule up the gangway, followed it aboard. Sandy trudged into the road. Eb's eyes followed somberly.

The water continued to rise and began to trickle into the yard. The voyagers hurried their preparations. Soon the dandelions which dotted the grass were no longer visible. By the time all the baggage the vessel could hold was aboard even the tallest weeds were obliterated, and the tops of the fence pickets appeared to be supports from which hung a muddy canopy. The passengers stood at the rope railing, and studied the ominous masses of cloud growing blacker and blacker in the western sky. As they watched the vessel shifted. A slow, almost imperceptible swaying followed.

Eb lifted a long pole, and thrust it experimentally over the side. "She's floating," he announced.

He replaced the pole on the deck, and minutely examining the hull to see if any leaks had developed, took a post at the stern. Here he waited until after midday when the picket fence was long submerged and he knew the water was deep enough to proceed. Leaning on the pole, he thrust the monster's nose past the giant beech that stood before the cottage, then turned the vessel sharply to glide between the flooded trees which marked the road.

"Where you going, Eb?" asked Judge, who with Ruby stood watching beside the lanky steersman. His thick brow was troubled. "This ain't the way to Granny Run, is it? Granny Run's over there." He pointed off in the direction of the darkening clouds.

"I ain't going to Granny Run for a while. I'm going down the road a piece." He continued to impel the craft forward until it was directly in front of Mr. Tackett's dilapidated cottage.

On the porch the old broommaker was standing in water that came up to his knees, hammering at a rickety skiff. On a flooded table near him were a few rusty tools and a battered phonograph.

Eb made the vessel fast to a tree.

Judge's fat eyes peered anxiously at the scudding horizon. "You ain't tying up here, are you, Eb?" he demanded. "Be better if we tried to get to Granny Run before night, wouldn't it? Hate to try to make it after dark. And can't tell what kind of storm we're going to have, neither. That sky ain't pretty."

"I got business to tend to here." Eb put down the pole, and cutting off a chunk from a plug of tobacco, thrust it into his mouth. He began to chew it solemnly, as he did so gazing fixedly at the old man and the skiff.

For some time Sandy continued his optimistic hammering. Satisfied at last, he climbed into the boat for a trial excursion. Seizing the oars, with surprising agility he began rowing along the line of golden tassels which marked the boundary of his corn patch. He turned to retrace his course, and smiled with triumph. "You'll see," he called out to his wife, who was looking on in derision. "I'll get to Granny Run before you will."

Almost as he spoke a gaping crack appeared in the bottom. A moment later the boat had sunk out of sight, and he was in water over his waist. Doggedly he floundered to the porch and climbed up the inundated stairs; defiantly he shook the water from his dripping clothes.

His wife shouted her indignation. He paid no attention, but looking about helplessly for a time, began making a raft of some floating soapboxes. This attempt, too, failed ignominiously. He went inside, reappearing soon after high up·in the house at the triangular window opening out of the minute attic. The watchers saw him set the phonograph on the sill and take a leisurely seat near by. He began placidly gazing out the window.

Judge's fat face showed his irritation. "Now what you doing, Sandy?" he shouted.

The old man did not change expression. "I'm just waiting. Waiting for something to happen."

"What'll happen?"

"Anything can happen at Caney Corners. Maybe a angel with a shiny dress and holding a harp'll come and write my name in a book."

Eb spat a withering chew into the water. "It was a trumpet he was holding," he grunted.

A long time the two men remained thus, like two sparring cats on guard for the other's next move, while the water climbed slowly up the walls of the house. The area of gloomy-fringed cloud in the distance widened.

Judge paced the deck, muttering to himself. "Look a-here, Sandy," he called at length. "There's a bad storm coming up and you're causing us all a heap of trouble. Right's right and a man's entitled to his opinions, I says. But this here is different. Ruby Corkell, he's a businessman, and he said it's a ark. I'm one of the leading citizens of this county, and I said it's a ark. You ain't nothing but a broommaker, Sandy. And what's a broommaker doing standing up against a businessman and a deputy county clerk?"

"I ain't standing up against you. I'm standing up against Eb."

Judge shrugged his shoulders. He turned to the statuesque pilot. "You're just wasting time, Eb. You better be getting over to Granny Run. We'll get caught in the storm sure if you don't."

"I ain't going. Not for a while anyways."

"I'm a officer of this county, Eb. Supposing I was to order you to go to Granny Run? What'd you say then?"

"I'd say that anybody didn't like my ark could get off and walk."

The plump Mrs. Corkell remembered her husband's clock, and tried to end the stalemate. "How about your phonograph, Sandy?" she trumpeted. "And them three records you got. That poet in the menagerie one particular where you can hear all them lions and tigers roaring. You want them to get all spoiled? I heard them saying down at Four Mile they don't make that roaring record no more."

Sandy's eyes grew wistful. "Rather lose a hundred phonographs than say what I didn't want to say. And water won't hurt the records none. They're wax."

The waves were now lapping about the tops of the lower windows. The blackness in the sky deepened. Thunder rolled dully. Sandy folded his feet beneath him as water began coming through the attic floor.

Eb loosed the vessel from her moorings, and poled twice back and forth before the house as though the movement might entice the other from his wet fastness. It had no effect.

Mrs. Tackett spoke to the pilot. "We been fooling with him long enough, Eb." She turned and faced her husband. "We're going now. You can come along or stay. But I been watching you and I've decided. If you don't come you won't never see me again. I married a man, I did, not a mule."

Sandy's snowy beard quivered. "You ain't going to leave me, are you, Nannie? You ain't going to leave your husband you been living with twenty-seven years? That ain't lawful, Nannie."

"Ain't lawful the way you're acting."

"But who'll put liniment on my back when I get my lumbago, and make them waffles for me? Ain't nobody in the whole United States makes waffles like you, Nannie."

The flattery left her unmoved. "You can get some other lady."

There was a pause. The old man surveyed the frigid visage of his wife, then searched the impassive countenance of the tall-hatted steersman. His head sunk in resignation. "I'll come," he sighed.

He stood erect and straddled the window. The boat bumped dully against the house, with the level of the deck a few feet below the sill. He stepped on board and started to hurry off to the shelter of the cabin.

Eb blocked his path again. "Just a minute," he said.

The old man gazed at him gloomily. "What you wanting?"

"You ain't said it yet. Is it a ark or is it just a shanty?"

Sandy stood hesitant. Suddenly he started to climb back into the window.

Mrs. Tackett caught him by the arm. "It is a ark now, ain't it, Sandy?" she demanded, with an acid smile which gave some indication of the fierce pressure her fingers were applying.

He saw there was no escape, and turning away his face, nodded in silent affirmation.

A few drops of rain splattered onto the deck.

Eb made the vessel fast to another tree. "Think we better tie up again for a few minutes till we see what the storm's going to do," he remarked. He turned to his newest passenger. "If you got one of them peppermint canes you're always a-chewing I'll take a piece. It's hard work a-running a ark."

Sandy took a sticky cane from a bag in his pocket, and broke off a fragment. Eb thrust it into his mouth. Soon after he went into the cabin, emerging with a bundle carefully wrapped in newspaper. He untied it and spread the contents near the tall strip of wood rising from the deck near the prow.

Ruby watched with curiosity. "What you got there, Eb?"

"What's it look like I got?"

"Looks like a flag, I guess."

"It is a flag. I'm going to run her up the mast."

Ruby grunted. "Noah didn't have no flag on his ark."

"No, nor there wasn't no United States then neither."

Scarcely was the flag fluttering from the staff when the storm wheeled out of the sky. A roaring wind plowed the water into angry waves. Rain battered the peaked roof and swept through the open windows. Lightning flashed in blinding streaks over the treetops. Thunder boomed continuously. Soon the tempest ended. But its cessation brought no clearing of the somber heavens, no lightening of the leaden, stifling air.

"Worse storm coming if I know anything about weather," Eb muttered to Ruby as he and the druggist stepped out from the cabin onto the streaming deck and loosened the mooring lines. "Can't wait here forever, though. It'll be pretty near night before we even get started."

He took up the steering pole again and gave a similar pole to Ruby. While Sandy and Judge emerged to watch, critical but silent, the two men began shoving the uncouth craft down the water. Their arms rose and fell mechanically. The vessel plowed through the murky waves.

An ugly splotch of purple behind them marked the setting of the sun. Night swallowed up the horizon. The poles continued to dip monotonously over the side. The mellow voice of Mrs. Corkell drifted out the black window. A dog in the cabin began to bay its hunger. A horse neighed startlingly. The sky brightened a little as the moon made a frightened attempt to emerge from a shrouding mass of clouds; darkened again as the endeavor failed. Ghostly shapes drifted past, bundles of brush and jagged trunks of trees; once there appeared what seemed to be a gigantic dunce cap which on coming nearer proved to be a haystack. Lightning began to flash again in the distance.

Judge drew out a thin stogie and struck a match. "Mighty dark, ain't it, Eb?" he queried. "How about having a lantern or something so we can see where we're going?"

Eb brushed the sweat from his forehead. "Noah didn't have no lantern on his ark. I don't need none neither."

"You put up a flag. Noah didn't have no flag."

"A flag's different. You got to have a flag."

A mist descended, smoky, impenetrable.

Judge chewed the end of his stogie nervously. "You sure you're going in the right direction, Eb? Mighty easy in the dark to get headed out to the river, and then where'd we be when she's flooding this way?"

"If you think you know better than me, you take the pole."

The mist cleared a little with a flurry of rain. The water

through which they were moving was sluggish. Ahead showed dancing flecks of white where drift was tumbling boisterously.

The steersman dropped the pole and brought the craft to a halt.

"Running mighty swift there, Eb," Judge remarked. "Must be the crick bed back of Jake Miner's place. Water always runs fast there even when there's just a little rain. It is the crick bed, ain't it?"

"It's the crick bed, alright."

"Think you can get across? Maybe you better try going up farther and crossing there. That's bad water, Eb. She's shooting down logs like they was kindling wood."

The pilot was about to make a sharp answer, when Ruby interrupted. "Judge is right, Eb," he declared persuasively. "Water's mighty swift. Think she can stand it?"

"When I build a ark, I build her."

He raised the pole and let the craft shoot forward. It touched the edge of the frothy water, gave a violent spin, and leaped downstream. The planking rumbled thunderously as some shadowy tree trunks hurled themselves against the hull. A candle was lighted inside the cabin. A frightened child began to cry. The boat swept on. A gigantic shadow detached itself from the blackness near the prow; a monstrous log, three times the size of the others, came hurtling down the current. Mightily Eb and Ruby, aided now by Judge and Sandy, struggled with the steering pole to swerve the vessel from its path. Their effort were unavailing. The log crashed explosively against the side. The vessel floundered onward, then drifted into quiet water.

Judge relinquished his grip on the pole. With Eb's permission he lit a lantern, and inspected the cavernous bottom. No break was visible anywhere in the stout-timbered sides.

He glowed with enthusiasm. "By God, she's a good . . . ark, Eb," he puffed. "By God, she's a fine ark."

The mist once more spread over the river. A pleasant sputtering began in the cabin; the smell of a lighted oil stove floated through the door. Mrs. Tackett followed the odor, bearing a tray of sizzling ham and eggs. To each man she gave a monstrous portion.

"Mighty smart of you to put that stove on your ark, Eb," she pronounced with all the flattery in her voice she could contrive.

He ate the food hungrily. "You know how to cook mighty smart on it."

"She makes better waffles," Sandy murmured.

Mrs. Tackett departed. The boat floated past a row of trees in whose upper branches crickets chirped faintly. An owl flew by, moaning desolately. The lightning shifted from the horizon to the sky overhead. A sudden furious gust of wind drove the boat off at a violent right angle. A second gust whirled it in a contrary direction. For a moment it wheeled and rolled with its prow facing every point of the compass. Then the blow lulled. The craft nosed on steadily through the mist.

Judge broke a stogie and gave half to Eb. "You sure you know where you're going, Eb?" he queried anxiously. "Looks to me maybe you got mixed up when the wind twisted us that way."

Eb smoked in silence. "I don't know no more than you where we're going now," he confessed at last, gloomily.

There was an odd grating noise under the bow. The vessel came to an abrupt stop. It began to move again; but the grating continued.

Ruby stabbed at the darkness with his pole. "Rocks sharp as razors," he muttered. "They'll rip the bottom right out her."

Eb's eyes strained to pierce the obscurity. "Must be that rocky land of Zeb Pike's," he answered. An ugly black line showed vaguely on both sides of the water. Eb guided the vessel through the narrow channel. A great stone, jagged, malevolent, appeared at the end of the passage; a swift current caught the boat and began dragging it forward. Eb hastily shifted his pole for a new maneuver. Before he could execute it, the vessel halted with a noise like the squeal of an irate pig. He opened a hatch, and taking the lantern, saw water rushing through an opened seam.

"It's a rock cut through," he announced.

He spread a plank over the break and commenced a steady hammering. As he toiled the child inside renewed its whimpering. A woman's voice, trying to soothe it, began to chant a dismal tune.

The board was nailed tight and the spurting water ceased.

Eb arose and took the oar again. The boat continued on its way.

Ruby walked to the new-made patch and examined it by the light of the flickering lantern. His eyes roamed the length of the grotesque hulk in admiration. "She's a good ark, Eb," he murmured. "Yep. She's a fine ark."

Eb wiped his perspiring forehead with his sleeve. He turned to Sandy. "I can use another hunk of that peppermint candy if you can spare it."

The old man nodded. "I got some mixed candy, too. Bought it down at that store at Goose Island when I was staying at my brother's. Maybe you'd rather have mixed candy."

"I'll take some mixed candy."

He selected a green gumdrop and popped it into his mouth. The others followed his example.

Judge sucked at a flinty butterball. "How about it now, Eb?" he demanded. "Maybe now you passed the rocks on Zeb's place you know where you're going?"

"Can't tell nothing in this mist."

The wind rose suddenly to hurricane violence. Lightning struck vividly in a clump of trees a hundred yards away. The men pressed against the wall, seizing projections in the wood to prevent their being blow away. The mist changed to a deluge. The surface of the water was churned into vast heaving billows. The craft lumbered and plunged giddily. Thunder rattled in terrifying volleys. Immense sheets of greenish flame swept from the waves to the sky. A windowpane shattered metallically. The light in the cabin and the lantern puffed out. The nasal voices of the women rose in a hymn.

By the intermittent flashes of lightning Eb could see the flag, ripping itself to tatters in the gale. Fighting his way forward, he hauled it down. A sudden shift of the storm sent the boat alongside a grove of poplars with tossing boughs upraised as though imploring mercy from their windy enemy. A giant tree toppled as they passed, splashing enormously into the waves. One massive bough fell squarely on the prow, and thrust it under the water. The stern, to equalize the weight, reared itself darkly above the swells. There was a confused clattering in the cabin, as those within lost their balance and furniture and shifting bundles bumped against the wall.

Eb seized an ax and began hacking fiercely at the imprisoning tree. The others snatched up sections of timber, and wielding them like crowbars, pried desperately. The vessel leaned heavily on its side as the current pressed against the uneven keel.

The women came darting out upon the deck. Seeing they could do nothing to aid, they returned to the interior and began a doleful prayer. The animals in their stalls stamped about in fright. The cow bellowed in quick, perfect timed intervals. The horses whinnied to each other eerily.

The list of the vessel grew worse. A box, dislodged from its resting place in the cabin, crashed through the window. The bits of broken glass sparkled like strange-shaped emeralds as the lightning touched their edges. The boat shuddered and appeared to be preparing a fatal dive. The men at the bow toiled herculeanly. The white chips from the ax sprayed like foam over the deck.

The cabin door was flung open again and Mrs. Ruby appeared clinging to the ghostly frame. Behind her the shapes of the other passengers were vaguely visible. "We're all ready to jump if we have to," she said coolly.

The wind, as in answer, roared contemptuously, tipping the vessel still further from the perpendicular.

Suddenly there was a loud crackling at the prow as the tree broke free. The vessel gave a prolonged shiver, and righting itself, shot down the water. Crazily it drove before the wind a few moments, then arrested its course as the tempest ended. Eb took up his pole and resumed his post at the stern. The rain ceased, and the smoky clouds opened to reveal a golden moon. The pilgrims gazed into the night. They were on a quiet, rippling ocean.

"Sure some storm, Eb," Judge puffed, as he took out another stogie. "And she sure was a fine ark to ride her out the way she done. "She's like iron."

Ruby nodded. "You said it right, Judge. She sure is a fine ark."

Judge peered off toward the moonlit horizon. "Ain't got no idea where we are, have you, Eb?"

"All water looks alike, don't it?" Eb took off his drenched coat and hung it on a nail. "If we had a dove on board I might send it out to see if there was land. Like Noah done. But I ain't got no dove."

Ruby took a reflective chew of tobacco. "Guess it wouldn't do no good sending out a chicken, would it?"

" 'Course it wouldn't. Wouldn't prove nothing. A chicken 'd drown before he got ten feet. I can send out a duck, though. Got some of 'em inside." He disappeared for a moment and returned with a quacking, feathery bundle. Walking to the bow he held it high in the air and let it fly out over the water. In an instant it had wheeled and come quacking back.

"Sign there ain't no land yet," Eb announced gravely.

The glimpse of the moon proved temporary. A new fog descended. Eb carried the duck to the bow again and tossed it forward. The bird quacked off into the darkness.

Fifteen minutes passed. The duck did not return.

"Guess he's lost, Eb." Judge blew a succession of melancholy smoke rings.

"Maybe. Or maybe he's done what I sent him out to do."

Ruby spat the last of his chew into the water. "I don't know about the rest of you but I'm getting hungry again," he declared.

"I got a coconut," Eb answered. "I'll fetch it. Looks like a good coconut, too. Bought it from a Italian come through on a wagon."

Ruby wiped his lips. "I knowed a Italian once. And all the time I knowed him I never could find out where he hid his knife. Smart, them Italians. Gimme the milk, will you?"

Eb was cracking the shell when there was a new scraping under the hull of the vessel. Its motion ceased.

"She's stuck again," Judge called in alarm.

Eb ran forward and peered over the rail. "It's land," he pronounced.

He leaped over the side, and making the vessel fast, plodded up the mud of a shadowy ridge. The other men followed. They reached the top. Here there was no mist. The moon glowed brightly over two squat church towers. Gasoline torches flamed smokily. A little distance away some sharp-silhouetted figures were erecting tents.

Judge sighed with beefy content. "It's Granny Run," he announced. "They're fixing a relief camp. We're all fine now." He took out a handkerchief and began drying his drenched hat. "I don't know what we'd have done without you, Eb. And I'll say to you what I said before. She was a fine ark you built. Bringing us through them logs and rocks and that storm and everything. A fine ark."

Ruby nodded in agreement. "I'll say it, too, way I said before, Eb. She's a mighty fine ark." He turned to the broom-maker, who was scraping the mud from his shoes against a stone. "How about you, Sandy? Ain't you saying nothing?"

The old man did not answer for a moment. Gravely he bent to tie one of the straggly bits of twine which served as his shoelaces, then stood erect and looked across the misty water.

"I'm saying it's a pretty good shanty," he said.

42

A 65 11

RIVER NOTE

Since Shantyboat Voyage was written, the towboat Sprague has been
retired, and given to the city of Vicksburg, Mississippi. Big Mama is
now anchored at the Vicksburg waterfront, doing duty as a steamboat
museum.

BLB

42